GOD'S CALENDAR
— FOR THE —
UNIVERSE

...unveiling the plan of ages

RAZAQ KABIRU BABATUNDE

Order this book online at www.trafford.com
or email orders@trafford.com

Most Trafford titles are also available at major online book retailers.

Printed in the United States of America.

ISBN: 978-1-4669-8300-7 (sc)
ISBN: 978-1-4669-8302-1 (hc)
ISBN: 978-1-4669-8301-4 (e)

Library of Congress Control Number: 2013903654

Trafford rev. 03/07/2013

 www.trafford.com

North America & international
toll-free: 1 888 232 4444 (USA & Canada)
phone: 250 383 6864 ♦ fax: 812 355 4082

DEDICATION

Rev. Chris Oyakhilome, PhD, president of Believers' LoveWorld Incorporated a.k.a. Christ Embassy; and his wife, Pastor Anita Oyakhilome.

ACKNOWLEDGMENTS

My great thanks go to God Almighty, the author and the finisher of his work. I appreciate great people like Pastor Francis Ben-Adesokan, Trina Hardy, Isokpehi Faith A, Adeshina Taiwo, Prince Adesegun Ogunlewe (the head of service of Lagos State Government), and Olorunfemi Adeola, among others. God has used them for my favor in all ramifications, particularly for the actualization of this book.

CONTENTS

PART ONE

CHAPTER ONE

DISPENSATIONS

And of the children of Issachar, which were men that had understanding of the times, to know what Israel ought to do; the heads of them were two hundred; and all their brethren were at their commandment.

—1 Chronicles 12:32

THE CHRISTIAN LIFE is a glorious life; it is a life of unending victory. But it is very glaring that not every Christian lives a continuous victorious life because many lack the knowledge of time. From the very beginning of the creation, God had been dealing with his creatures according to his own stipulated way of life for them, and it is the responsibility of the creature to learn the time and function consistently in the context of the time of God. In 1 Chronicles 12:32, God talks about the children of Issachar who understood the times and knew what Israel ought to do at a particular time. "And of the children of Issachar, which were men that had understanding of the times, to know what Israel ought to do. "This shows that you can't just do anything the way you feel; if you must live a glorious life and not be a victim of the strategies of the devil, your way of life has to be consistent with the time in God's calendar.

God is perfect in plans and strategies; it is part of his awesome nature and supremacy. Therefore, any man that must work with him must understand his calendar. Many Christians have missed this simple point, and they are paying dearly for it. Many Christians are poor, sick, and dying because of their lack of understanding of time. The same thing is applicable to the unsaved ones that decided not to give their lives to Christ.

There is so much chaos in the world because the world is full of confused people. This is the reason people stand against the gospel. It is obvious that all the terrorist attacks all around the world are because of Christianity. The United States of America is hated passionately and attacked by Islamic terrorists particularly because of Christianity. The same is going on in Nigeria where scores of churches were bombed and many Christians were killed. Lots of the Christians' properties were destroyed.

Another laughable scenario is the scientific forecast that even predicted that the world will end in December 2012. All the confusion in the world today is a result of the fact that they lack knowledge of the timing of God. God is so good, and he is not an author of confusion.

I have therefore made it incumbent on myself to unveil the timing of God in this book for the believers, and the journey will have to start from this chapter, subtitled "Dispensations." Having gone through the contents of the book, it will be very impossible for some folks to understand the truth that is shared in this book without fully understanding the nine dispensations as they are carefully elucidated in this chapter.

Someone may ask, what is *dispensation*? *Dispensation* from the biblical point of view means *administration*. The Greek word for dispensation is *oikonoma*, which means "administration of a household or estate." It can also be referred to as stewardship.

This is telling us that God is the oikonomia of the heavens and earth. He did not just create the heavens and the earth and left them unmanaged. He is in the job of managing the heavens and earth, including the entirety of creatures in them, and administrating the whole universe. He has his program and schemes that we must learn and master in order to take advantage of the benefit of the dispensation that we belong.

The word *generation* is used in the Old Testament instead of *dispensation*, but the two words were used for the same purpose. They were used to express the fact that God had prepared the activities of the heavens and the earth in segments.

The Hebrew word for *generation* is *dowr*, which means "a revolution of time points to the case of suspension or living one age/generation and proceeding to another generation." Since the word *generation* (*dowr*) can mean as a *revolution*, it means "a great change of government," most of the time in a violent way—not forgetting that *government*, *administration*, and *dispensation* are synonymous.

Therefore, the words *generation* and *dispensation* are synonymous. It must be noted that God is always conscious of the matter of generation/ dispensation because that is the epicenter of his dealing with all creatures.

Genesis 7:1, "And the LORD said unto Noah, Come thou and all thy house into the ark; for thee have I seen righteous before me in this generation." The Hebrew word used for *generation* in this scripture is *dowr*, which shows that there had been a generation before that generation that Noah lived. If there had been no other generation before and after Noah's generation, God could have used *the* instead of *this*. And it must be noted that God was not talking about *generation* according to family, history, or natural birth; the Hebrew word for *generation* according to family history or natural birth is *towledwth*. This does not have anything to do with the calendar of God and his administration; *towledwth* is used in Genesis 2:4 when the Bible says, "These are the generations of the heavens and of the earth when they were created, in the day that the LORD God made the earth and the heavens." The choice of word of *generation* does not have anything to do with dispensation. *Generation* in this scripture is talking about history, birth, and/or family, which have nothing to do with our subject matter. Our subject matter here is talking about dispensation, a revolution of time—that is, ages or generations according to the plan of God.

The heavens and the earth from the very beginning to eternity have been preprogrammed into nine glaring and well-stipulated dispensations. The nine dispensations are as follows:

Dispensation of Angel
Dispensation of Innocence
Dispensation of Conscience
Dispensation of Human Government
Dispensation of Promise
Dispensation of Law
Dispensation of Grace
Dispensation of Divine Government
Dispensation of Eternity

Dispensation of Angel

The first dispensation is the dispensation of angel. God preexisted the beginning, and in Genesis 1:1, God created the heavens and the earth and made them to be inhabited. "For thus saith the LORD that created the heavens; God himself that formed the earth and made it; he hath established it, he created it not in vain, he formed it to be inhabited: I am the LORD; and there is none else." The New American Bible presents it in the following way: "For thus says the Lord, who created the heavens [He is the God who formed the earth. He established it and did not create it as a wasted place but formed it to be inhabited]" (Isa. 45:18). This tells us that the initial creation of Genesis 1:1 included angels and some other creatures like animals. Dinosaurs and mammoths were created in the angelic dispensation. The earth was inhabited; it was not created void and formless like a wasted place full of darkness.

For better understanding, it must be understood that the creation from Genesis 1:6-31 was not the initial creation of God;

it was actually a re-creation. The first creation started with the angelic dispensation, and it was dominated and ruled by angels. Lucifer was an archangel and lived in the earth and had the capability to go from the earth to heaven to minister to God.

If you study Ezekiel 28:13, you will discover that Lucifer was created on the earth, and the account of his fall in Isaiah 14:12-14 shows that he lived and ruled on the earth before he committed high treason against God and before he was felled. Ezekiel 28 says that Lucifer was the anointed cherub, meaning that Lucifer was anointed on the earth by God to expand, spread, and have dominion.

The anointing gave him the ability to have dominion on earth and to expand and spread out. God anointed Lucifer to have dominion on the face of the earth because he would not have anointed him to expand his kingdom in heaven. It is real that God created the angels to function under him. He was also able to go from earth to heaven in the presence of God because of his angelic nature.

The dispensation of angel came to an end when Lucifer committed high treason against God and fell. The revolution took place on earth because Lucifer was the king of the earth at the time. The earth came into chaos, and that dispensation came to an end, and then God started the re-creation of the earth in Genesis 1:6 in order to start another dispensation.

Dispensation of Innocence

The second dispensation fully started from Genesis 2:15 when God put Adam into the Garden of Eden. Adam and Eve were the only two of mankind that enjoyed the dispensation of innocence. They lived as innocents that could do nothing right or wrong. They were innocents by nature. They could have done what we regard as sin today but could not be made as sinners because they were not obliged to keep any law. If they had lived without eating from the tree of knowledge of good and evil, they would still be as innocent as God. In the dispensation of innocence, they had the human nature, and it can also be called the Adamic nature, which tells us that human nature is the nature of innocence. They lived in perfect harmony with God. They could do nothing right or wrong. They just lived and pleased God. They did not need faith to please God.

The dispensation of innocence came to an end in Genesis 3:21. They were still under the dispensation of innocence even when they had eaten the fruit; they walked out of the dispensation of innocence when God pronounced judgment over them and made garments of skin for them; that was the last physical encounter Adam and Eve had with God.

Dispensation of Conscience

The third dispensation was the dispensation of conscience. This dispensation started from the fall of man through Adam. When man had fallen and been sent out of the Garden of Eden, they started living as sinners; they actually became sinners subject to the dictates and guidance of their consciences. They were spiritually dead and far from God. They only had their senses as their teachers; their experiences were their best teachers unlike us, the Christians that have the Holy Ghost as our best teacher.

There was no law for them to live by; they did what their consciences approved and tried to avoid what their consciences disapproved. We have to understand that their consciences could not necessarily approve good things because their spirit could not receive counsel from God; their approvals and disapprovals were characterized with evil because they were naturally sinners.

This is the dispensation I call the dispensation of assumption. The Bible shows that this dispensation was the most sinful dispensation; this is the reason God destroyed the earth with flood. It was only Noah and his household that escaped the flood because Noah found favor in the eyes of God. The Bible says, "But Noah found grace in the eyes of the LORD" (Gen. 6:8).

Salvation under this dispensation as by God's favor was by faith in what God said (Gen. 6:13-14, 7:5; Heb. 11:6-7) *and* by works through the right offerings (Gen. 4:1-7). The good example of salvation under this dispensation is located in Genesis 6:8 when the scriptures say, "But Noah found grace in the eyes of the LORD." The Hebrew word for favor is *chen*, which means *graciousness* (i.e., subjective [kindness, favor] or objective [beauty]—*favor, gracious, pleasant, precious, well favored*). This shows that God favored Noah to be used as a vessel by God to preserve the world.

People's sins could only be forgiven and covered by animal sacrifices in spite of the fact that God is full of favor. People had to make animal sacrifices for their sins to be forgiven and covered. Hebrews 11:4 says, "By faith Abel offered unto God a more excellent sacrifice than Cain, by which he obtained witness that he was righteous, God testifying of his gifts: and by it he being dead yet speaketh." However, the people's sins' penalties could not be taken away by those sacrifices but were actually covered with the blood of the animals. "For the law having a shadow of good things to come, and not the very image of the things, can never with those sacrifices which they offered year by year continually make the comers thereunto perfect. For then would they not have ceased to be offered? because that the worshippers once purged should have had no more conscience of sins. But in those sacrifices there is a remembrance again made of sins every year. For it is not possible that the blood of bulls and of goats should take away sins. Wherefore when he cometh into the world, he saith, Sacrifice and offering thou wouldest not, but a body hast thou prepared me: In burnt offerings and sacrifices for sin thou hast had no pleasure . . . And every priest standeth daily ministering and offering oftentimes the same sacrifices, which can never take away sins:" (Heb. 10:1-4, 6, 11).

However this dispensation came to an end because of men's wicked deeds and evil thoughts; thus, righteous God brought great judgment on the earth and the people by destroying both men and beasts with flood. The Bible says, "And GOD saw that the wickedness of man was great in the earth, and that every imagination of the thoughts of his heart was only evil continually. And it repented the LORD that he had made man on the earth, and it grieved him at his heart. And the LORD said, I will destroy man whom I have created from the face of the earth; both man, and beast, and the creeping thing, and the fowls of the air; for it repenteth me that I have made them" (Gen. 6:5-7).

Dispensation of Human Government

The fourth dispensation was the dispensation of human government. This is the patriarchal age. It was between the periods of Noah to when Abraham was seventy-five years old. It was an aggregate of 425 years. "And Noah builded an altar unto the LORD; and took of every clean beast, and of every clean fowl, and offered burnt offerings on the altar" and "And the LORD came down upon mount Sinai, on the top of the mount: and the LORD called Moses up to the top of the mount; and Moses went up" (Gen. 8:20; Exod. 19:20). It is the dispensation between the above stated Genesis 8:20 and Exodus 19:20. It was from the end of the Noahic flood to the giving of the Ten Commandments.

At that period of time, men lived and were governed according to their own constitution, their own policies. Remember, men were far from God. God could not directly influence their government or way of life.

They lived as they wanted; they chose their own kind of government. The weak run to the physically powerful for protection, but the strong take advantage of the weak. Though God was highly interested in the existence of mankind, he could not control and govern them because they were under the authority of the devil; thus, God deliberately suspended that dispensation by calling Abraham out of his father's land, but this had to go though a process. Therefore, he introduced the dispensation of promise.

Salvation during the period of the dispensation of human government was by divine favor and faith in the promise of God. The Bible describes the act of salvation under this dispensation in the following scripture: "After these things the word of the LORD came unto Abram in a vision, saying, Fear not, Abram: I am thy shield, and thy exceeding great reward. And Abram said, Lord GOD, what wilt thou give me, seeing I go childless, and the steward of my house is this Eliezer of Damascus? And Abram said, Behold, to me thou hast given no seed: and, lo, one born in my house is mine heir. And, behold, the word of the LORD came unto him, saying, This shall not be thine heir; but he that shall come forth out of thine own bowels shall be thine heir. And he brought him forth abroad, and said, Look now toward heaven, and tell the stars, if thou be able to number them: and he said unto him, So shall thy seed be. And he believed in the LORD; and he counted it to him for righteousness" (Gen. 15:1-6), and they had fellowship with God through the offering of sacrifices.

During this dispensation, sins were forgiven by the offering of sacrifices, but sin penalties were not taken away, and the offered blood of the animal sacrificed was just to cover their sins for a while. God had to introduce the dispensation of promise to begin the process of salvation through Christ Jesus.

Dispensation of Promise

The fifth dispensation is the dispensation of promise. This dispensation started from Abraham's call at the age of seventy-five. God found a man as a custodian of the promise in Abraham. God chose Abraham as a means of reaching the world. God promised Abraham to bless him and make him a blessing to the entire human creation.

God actually determined to bless all mankind, but he couldn't bless them because he knew that they could not be blessed without their attention on God and consciousness on the blessing. So he first of all blessed Abraham that had enough faith to receive God's blessing and influenced the world through him.

Under the dispensation of promise, only Abraham and his biological children enjoyed God's blessing. Lot and his family took the advantages of the blessing of Abraham because he followed him when he was called out of his fatherland but later lost everything he got when he left Abraham (Gen. 13). Every man that came across Abraham knew that he was blessed by the Lord.

When Abraham died in 1991 BC, the dispensation of promise did not end because Abraham was not the original target of the dispensation; the original target of the dispensation of promise was the whole planet earth through the seed of Abraham. God continued that dispensation with Abraham's biological children: Isaac to Jacob to all the Israelites. For the benefit of the fulfillment of the promise, God changed Jacob's name to Israel. When the Israelites lived in Egypt, they were still under the dispensation of promise. This is the main source of their victory. God called them his own people because of his promise that worked with a covenant.

Moses also lived and started his ministry under the dispensation of promise. God was able to use Moses greatly because he came from the tribe of Israel and functioned under the promise of God. Moses delivered the children of Israel from Egypt under the dispensation promise, and the dispensation came to an end when God gave law to Moses to rule his people. The dispensation wouldn't have to come to an end if the law was not given. Thus, the dispensation of promise came to an end when God gave law exclusively for the people under the dispensation of promise. The introduction of law was the introduction of the dispensation of law, and the children of Israel were the only set people that functioned under the dispensation of law because Gentiles were without law. At this period, the Gentiles were out of the calendar of God. They were without God in the world.

Dispensation of Law

The sixth dispensation is the dispensation of law. This is the most recognized dispensation among many Christians and Jews today. This dispensation was a remarkable dispensation in the history of mankind because God had the opportunity of relating to and walking among men, particularly the children of Israel. God used law as a tool of relating with the children of Israel.

The law was not like the rules of the consciences of men that were ruled by the satanic nature and perfected by the unholy human government. The law was spiritual; it was given to guide the activities of the children of Israel. The law made God's mind known to the people. The children of Israel had God as their father. The Gentiles were alienated from God; they lived in darkness. The Gentiles were without God, strangers to the family of God. They did not have a job in obeying God.

In Leviticus 26:11-12, God said, "And I will set my tabernacle among you: and my soul shall not abhor you. And I will walk among you, and will be your God, and ye shall be my people." God started his relationship with the Israelites in the dispensation of law though aimed at having a relationship with both the Jews and the Gentiles.

The dispensation of law came with the spiritual wall of hostility that separated Jews from the Gentiles, and that wall reflected in their physical relationship. But God, who is rich in mercy, wanted the whole world to benefit from his unending grace; he broke that wall of hostility that separated the Jews from the Gentiles. "For he is our peace, who hath made both one, and hath broken down the middle wall of partition between us; Having abolished in his flesh the enmity, even the law of commandments contained in ordinances; for to make in himself of twain one new man, so making peace; And that he might reconcile both unto God in one body by the cross, having slain the enmity thereby: And came and preached peace to you which were afar off, and to them that were nigh. For through him we both have access by one Spirit unto the Father" (Eph. 2:14-18). God loves the whole world, but the law was only capable of accommodating the children of Israel. Ephesians 2:11-12 points out that the Gentiles were uncircumcised; they were separated from God, excluded from the citizenship of Israel, and were foreigners to the covenant of the dispensation of promise—without hope and without God in the world.

The dispensation of law was a shadow of the dispensation that the church lives in. The dispensation of law was not the reality of the plan of God; it was just a test run of the reality that is the dispensation of grace. It came and went, but because the dispensation of law was the dispensation that recorded the manifestation of Deity among his people, many Christians had decided to settle for the law (shadow), which is not the reality. Many Christians are living their lives in the consciousness of the dispensation of law that is not even again in existence.

Without any doubt, the dispensation of law was actually great; it was neither for the Gentiles nor for the church. It must be clearly stated that the dispensation of law came to an end at the resurrection of our Lord Jesus Christ. Though Jesus lived in the dispensation of law, his resurrection eradicated the dispensation of law and ushered in the dispensation of grace.

In the latter period of the dispensation of law, Jesus was born, lived, and functioned perfectly according to the requirement of the law. He went to the cross as the sacrifice for the sins of the people under the law and those who were not under the law (both Jews and Gentiles). Having gone to the cross as a sacrifice for the whole world, the requirement of the law was met. Jesus abolished the law in his flesh (Eph. 2:14) and ushered in the dispensation of grace.

Dispensation of Grace

The seventh dispensation is the dispensation of grace. This dispensation came into being by the resurrection of our Lord Jesus. The dispensation of grace is the major vision of God. God started the journey of the dispensation of grace with Abraham.

When God called him out of his father's household, the land that God was talking about was not the Canaan land.

Canaan land was just a shadow of the real Promised Land—just as the temple's holiest of holies was a shadow of the most holy place in heaven. The Bible tells us that Abraham looked for a city, the Promised Land that we will live in, whose architect and builder is God (Heb. 11: 10).

By faith, he (Abraham) sojourned in the land of promise as in a strange country, dwelling in tabernacles with Isaac and Jacob—the heirs with him of the same promise. "For he looked for a city which hath foundations, whose builder and maker is God." The Message version presents it in a more clear way in this manner: "By an act of faith he lived in the country promised him, lived as a stranger camping in tents. Isaac and Jacob did the same, living under the same promise. Abraham did it by keeping his eye on an unseen city with real, eternal foundations—the City designed and built by God."

The description of the city shows that the city was in the spirit realm; the city is Zion, and it came to reality when Jesus resurrected. We live in that city now. That is where every Christian belongs. We did not walk into the city; we were born in there when we gave our lives to Christ. We were translated into the kingdom of God at the point of the spiritual birth; if you are born again, you are born into the city (Zion) of God.

Hebrews 12:22-24 tells us that if you are born again, you have come to Mount Zion—the heavenly Jerusalem and the city of the living God—and to the thousands upon thousands of angels in joyful assembly at the church of the firstborn. "But ye are come unto mount Sion, and unto the city of the living God, the heavenly Jerusalem, and to an innumerable company of angels, To the general assembly and church of the firstborn, which are written in heaven, and to God the Judge of all, and to the spirits of just men made perfect, And to Jesus the mediator of the new covenant, and to the blood of sprinkling, that speaketh better things than that of Abel."

The Message version presents it as the following: "You've come to Mount Zion, the city where the living God resides. The invisible Jerusalem is populated by throngs of festive angels and Christian citizens. It is the city where God is Judge, with judgments that make us just. You've come to Jesus, who presents us with a new covenant, a fresh charter from God. He is the Mediator of this covenant. The murder of Jesus, unlike Abel's—a homicide that cried out for vengeance—became a proclamation of grace."

The dispensation of grace is real in Zion just as the dispensation of law was real to the children of Israel only. In other words, though we are in the dispensation of grace now, not everyone is enjoying it because not everyone is in the city where the dispensation is real.

If you are not born again, even though you are a Jew, you cannot function in the dispensation of grace. The Israelites functioned under the dispensation of law because they were biologically born as children of Israel. In the same way, you can function under the dispensation of grace if you are spiritually born by God in Zion.

The dispensation of grace is also the generation of kings, priests, and holy people (Rev. 5:10, Rom. 1:17, and 1 Pet. 2:9). God carefully set up Zion to be dominated by the seed of Abraham. When God talked about the establishment of his covenant with Abraham's seed, he was actually talking about Christ, which includes Jesus and every born-again believer.

We know very well that we are not set right with God by rule-keeping but only through personal faith in Jesus Christ. How do we know? We tried it—and we had the best system of rules the world has ever seen! Convinced that no human being can please God by self-improvement, we believed in Jesus as the Messiah so that we might be set right before God by trusting in the Messiah, not by trying to be good (Gal. 2:16).

Abraham's natural children enjoyed the dispensation of law, and the spiritual seeds of Abraham have the dispensation of grace. The dispensation of grace is the dispensation of the new creatures

(2 Cor. 5:17). Jesus said you must be born again; thus, you can enjoy the grace. If you are not born again, you are not under the dispensation of grace even though you are alive now. Though Jesus's death made grace available for the whole world, you have to adopt that fact in your life by being born again before you can enjoy the grace of God.

The importance of this is that God is not after what you do or what you do not do; he is after your place of belonging. In other words, he can only be identified with you if you are under his grace. If you are not under his grace, you are already condemned. That is the reason he gave his nature to everyone under the dispensation of grace so he will be able to have a father-and-children relationship with us. The grace of God is what makes us victorious always and enjoy a divine hearth.

The rapture of the church will take place under the dispensation of grace, and it is only we that are under the dispensation of grace by the agency of the new birth that will rapture with Jesus Christ. We, the church, will be raptured and be in heaven for seven years. The world will be in chaos and under great tribulation for seven years. Those last seven years will be characterized with satanic programming under the rule of the Antichrist. At this time also, the dispensation of grace will still be intact, but the church, the first beneficiaries of the grace, will be in heaven.

Our last seven years of the dispensation of grace will be spent in heaven though the grace will extend to the earth for the benefit of those that will die in the tribulation. The dispensation of grace will end at the Second Coming of Christ with the church. The end of the dispensation of grace will not be as a result of its failure but to give room for the continuation of God's plan, basically for the dispensation of divine government.

Dispensation of Divine Government

The eighth dispensation is the dispensation of divine government. This is the dispensation we are going to rule and reign in with our Lord Jesus for a millennium on this earth. In the dispensation of divine government, there will be no president or any political leader. Jesus will rule the world; there will be no ethnic, tribal, or national difference. We will have the culture of Zion. People that will come out of the tribulation will learn how to live in Zion with us.

Jesus is the supreme head of the dispensation of divine government, and the church will be the kings and priests of the dispensation. "And hast made us unto our God kings and priests: and we shall reign on the earth" (Rev. 5:10). Jesus is the King of kings. In this dispensation, there will be no satanic influence; the world will be at peace because Satan would have been imprisoned by then.

The dispensation of divine government will end at the end of one thousand years. At the concluding period of this dispensation, Satan will be released to tempt those that escaped the tribulation and their children. Then, there will be the final judgment. Immediately after the final judgment, there will be the dispensation of eternity.

Dispensation of Eternity

The ninth dispensation will be the last dispensation. The dispensation of eternity will usher in a new heaven and a new earth. The headquarters of the dispensation of eternity will be New Jerusalem. The throne of God will be in New Jerusalem. In this dispensation, there will be total victory in the presence of God Almighty. The dispensation of eternity will be from the end of the great white throne of judgment to the eternity future.

This period is located in the Bible between Revelation 21:1 when the Bible says, "And I saw a new heaven and a new earth: for the first heaven and the first earth were passed away; and there was no more sea," and Revelation 22:5 that says, "And there shall be no night there; and they need no candle, neither light of the sun; for the Lord God giveth them light: and they shall reign for ever and ever."

The dispensation of eternity will be a period of timeless reign because we will be in the timeless zone where God dwells. There will be three distinct sets of people reigning with the Lord in eternity. The Bible shows the three distinct people in 1 Corinthians 10:32 when it says, "Give none offence, neither to the Jews, nor to the Gentiles, nor to the church of God."

    i. The church of Jesus Christ (Christians)
    ii. The Jews (the nation of Israel)
    iii. The Gentiles (people of the nations that are not in the nation of Israel and are Christians)

The three classes of people will go to different places: new heaven and new earth—New Jerusalem for the Christians and a lake of fire for the unsaved.

This can also be referred to as the "dispensation of the fullness of times" because the dispensation has no end. Ephesians 1:10 says "that in the dispensation of the fulness of times he might gather together in one all things in Christ, both which are in heaven, and which are on earth; even in him."

This is a dispensation that will not require preaching of the gospel or the winning of souls. This is the dispensation of perfect rest in Christ Jesus. This is the period when no sin will be found in the world; nobody will sin because the devil, the tempter, will no longer be able to tempt anyone to sin because he will be in the lake of fire, being tormented forever. "And the devil that deceived them was cast into the lake of fire and brimstone, where the beast and the false prophet are, and shall be tormented day and night forever and ever" (Rev. 20:10).

More so, nobody will die in this dispensation because there will be no more death; the Bible says, "The last enemy that shall be destroyed is death" (1 Cor. 15:26).

All the discussed dispensations above are actually the keys to all of what you are going to learn in this book. The complete knowledge of the nine dispensations is very important for all Christians because that is what teaches us about God and his programs in the past, now, and future. "And that from a child thou hast known the holy scriptures, which are able to make thee wise unto salvation through faith which is in Christ Jesus. All scripture is given by inspiration of God, and is profitable for doctrine, for reproof, for correction, for instruction in righteousness: That the man of God may be perfect, thoroughly furnished unto all good works" (2 Tim. 3:15-17). This book will change lives as you continue reading it because it will unveil to you the reality of the work and acts of God on the face of the earth till the eternity.

CHAPTER TWO

THE PRE-ADAMIC

For thus saith the LORD that created the heavens; God himself that formed the earth and made it; he hath established it, he created it not in vain, he formed it to be inhabited: I am the LORD; and there is none else.

—Isaiah 45:18

ADAM WAS THE first man who dwelt on the earth, but biblical records show that there was a kingdom on this earth before the creation of Adam; that kingdom is what I refer to as the pre-Adamic kingdom.

When God created the heavens and the earth in the very beginning, Isaiah 45:18 shows that God made the earth to be inhabited in the very beginning. The Hebrew word that was used for *inhabited* is *yashab*, which means "to dwell in." In other words, the earth was occupied though not by human beings but by other living creatures. This shows that the creation in Genesis 1:1 was not the initial creation; the earth was originally populated, full of some entities, and the earth was ruled by one unique being—Lucifer—before the record of Genesis 1.

Though the Bible gives very little information about the pre-Adamic kingdom, the Holy Spirit is able to give light into the subject matter by revelation, using the available scriptures as a background to unveil the reality of the pre-Adamic kingdom. God is actually giving us an insight into the reality so the church will not live in the dark.

It is impossible to talk about the pre-Adamic kingdom without talking about the origin of Lucifer because he is the epicenter of that era before he committed high treason against God. This will definitely help us with the background understanding of God and the new creation.

The world of God shows that he was created on the earth and lived on the earth; then we have to know why he was evacuated from the earth and why human beings were created to occupy the earth instead of Lucifer. This book is designed to unveil this because most of the time, the challenge of many Christians is the problem of a lack of knowledge about the origin of Lucifer; that is why they tend to fear and respect him because they do not know how useless and powerless he is.

THE LUCIFER

When God created the heavens and the earth, he created angels and animals. Archaeological reports tell us that dinosaurs and mammoths lived on this very earth several millions of years before Adam. Those animals were in existence; they definitely lived in the earth during the pre-Adamic kingdom. The pre-Adamic kingdom was fashioned with God's wisdom and excellent beauty.

The earth was populated by several creatures in which Lucifer was their overall head. He was a chief angel; he had the ability to transport himself from the earth to heaven to render services to God, but the throne of Lucifer was on the earth as the major dominant of the earth. One third of the angels of God were directly under him to render service to God and adore his glory.

CREATION OF LUCIFER

The creation of the beautiful Lucifer also reveals that he lived on the earth during the pre-Adamic kingdom. Ezekiel 28:13 states,

> Thou hast been in Eden the garden of God; every precious stone was thy covering, the sardius, topaz, and the diamond, the beryl, the onyx, and the jasper, the sapphire, the emerald, and the carbuncle, and gold: the workmanship of thy tabrets and of thy pipes was prepared in thee in the day that thou wast created.

This is an account of the creation of Lucifer. God created him on this earth and put him in the Garden of Eden. His beauty was perfect. He was dressed in splendor and was created out of the combinations of many stones, and it must be noted that all those stones were precious stones; that is why he was beautiful. It must also be noted that the stones that God used to create him were gathered on the earth—not in heaven.

I would like to examine all the stones that God used to create Lucifer respectively to establish the fact that he was created on the earth and to ascertain his beauty.

- o Ruby: A valuable, transparent deep-red precious stone.
- o Topaz: Any of various yellow gems.
- o Emerald: A rich green gemstone.
- o Chrysolite: A green-colored and sometimes transparent gem.
- o Onyx: A limestone similar to marble and with layers of color.
- o Jasper: An opaque and many-shaded variety of quartz that when polished is made into a variety of ornamental articles and jewelry.
- o Sapphire: A transparent blue precious stone.

o   Turquoise: An opaque greenish-blue mineral that is valued as a gem.

o   Beryl: A usually green precious stone.

All the above discussed stones were fashioned and used by God to create Lucifer. Without any doubt, it is very obvious that Lucifer lived on earth before Adam, and he was created by stones that were gathered on the earth, which explains the reality of the pre-Adamic kingdom on the face of the earth.

The understanding of the pre-Adamic kingdom is the only means of knowing the origin of Satan and the evil spirits that are on the earth today. They were in existence in the pre-Adamic kingdom though they were not known as Satan/the devil or evil spirits during the pre-Adamic kingdom because they were created to service God. The present devil was a chief angel with numerous angels under him. Satan/Devil is his present official name; he took over that name when he fell, and the angels under him also fell. Isaiah 14:12-15 has the update of Lucifer's fall.

How art thou fallen from heaven, O Lucifer, son of the morning! how art thou cut down to the ground, which didst weaken the nations! For thou hast said in thine heart, I will ascend into heaven, I will exalt my throne above the stars of God: I will sit also upon the mount of the congregation, in the sides of the north: I will ascend above the heights of the clouds; I will be like the most High. thou shalt be brought down to hell, to the sides of the pit. They that see thee shall narrowly look upon thee, and consider thee, saying, Is this the man that made the earth to tremble, that did shake kingdoms; That made the world as a wilderness, and destroyed the cities thereof; that opened not the house of his prisoners? All the kings of the nations, even all of them, lie in glory, every one in his own house. But thou art cast out of thy grave like an abominable branch, and as the raiment of those that are slain, thrust through with a sword, that go down to the stones of the pit; as a carcase trodden under feet."

I will also like to present the New International Version of the scripture below for a glaring presentation of the message:

How you have fallen from heaven, O morning star, son of the dawn! You have been cast down to the earth, you who once laid low the nations! You said in your heart,

"I will ascend to heaven;
I will raise my throne above the stars of God;
I will sit enthroned on the mount of assembly, on the utmost heights of the sacred mountain.
I will ascend above the tops of the clouds;
I will make myself like the Most High."

But you are brought down to the grave, to the depths of the pit. Those who see you stare at you, they ponder your fate: "Is this the man who shook the earth and made kingdoms tremble, the man who made the world a desert, who overthrew its cities and would not let his captives go home?" All the kings of the nations lie in state, each in his own tomb. But you are cast out of your tomb like a rejected branch; you are covered with the slain, with those pierced by the sword, those who descend to the stones of the pit. Like a corpse trampled underfoot.

This is the brief record of Lucifer's life on the earth before his fall. The scriptures say that "how you have fallen from heaven, o morning star, son of the dawn." This passage tells that Lucifer was cast down from heaven to the earth; this shows the immediate action that God took when Lucifer committed high treason against him. But that does not mean that Lucifer was living permanently in heaven at that time; he lived on the earth but had the power to go to heaven whenever he chose. Remember, he could enter heaven as a messenger of God. The clause "Cast him from heaven to the earth" talks about when he was sent back to the earth violently to prevent him from causing chaos in heaven.

If you examine the very sin that Lucifer committed, we will clearly know who he really was and where he lived before he fell. The account of his sin was gathered from the thought of his heart when he said, "I will ascend to heaven; I will raise my throne above the stars of God; I will *sit* enthroned on the mount of assembly, on the tops of the clouds; I will make myself like most High;" (Isa. 14). This reveals the dwelling place of Lucifer was under the heavens. That is the reason he said, "I will ascend to heaven." If he resided in heaven, he would not have to wish to ascend to heaven. He also said, "I will raise my throne above the stars of God"; this shows that the dominion of Lucifer was below the atmospheric heaven where the stars belong.

Some folks had misinterpreted that passage by saying that Lucifer was referring to the angels, but the scriptures show that the word *stars* in the scripture do not refer to angels; it is actually talking about the stars in the atmospheric heaven because the Hebrew word that was used there is *kowkab*, which actually means "the shining in the sky"—meaning that the dominion and abode of Lucifer was below the stars that shine in the sky. He also thought of setting his throne on the mount of assembly. He said he would set his throne on the mount. The Hebrew word for *mount* there is *har*, meaning as a shorter form of *mountain* or *range of hills*, which is located in the earth. When he said, "I will sit enthroned on the mount of assembly," the Hebrew word for *assembly* is *mowed*, which means "the place of appointment." The mount of assembly in the scripture talks about the gathering of the holy angels. Lucifer wanted to take over the place of God. Lucifer thought about the extension of his dominion to the clouds to be like Jehovah and tried to materialize his thought.

Lastly, he wanted to make himself "like the most high." The Hebrew for *most high* is *eloywn*, meaning "the supreme, the most high, or the highest in respect to God." He wanted to dethrone God and enthrone himself.

Thus, Lucifer dwelt on the earth and was a chief angel; he dominated all other creatures in the earth at that period of time. With the dug-up history, archaeological researchers help in this study when they report the discovery of dinosaur and mammoth bones. It was reported that dinosaurs were in existence millions of years ago, but they are now extinct. Dinosaurs were very large animals that could not possibly live with human beings because of their dangerous natures. They are very terrible animals, huge and hairy like elephants. Mammoths are said to be extremely large. Those kinds of animals could only live with the angels.

Lucifer was a created being with angelic power; God did not create him as we know him today. God did not create Satan; he created Lucifer. He became Satan/the devil when he declared his five wills in his heart. The most terrible among them is when he said, "I will make myself like most high." He knew God and worked for God. He knew his majesty; thus, he decided to dethrone God because he desired his glory and majesty. God responded in his majesty and said in Ezekiel: 28:16-17,

> By the multitude of thy merchandise they have filled the midst of thee with violence, and thou hast sinned: therefore I will cast thee as profane out of the mountain of God: and I will destroy thee, O covering cherub, from the midst of the stones of fire. Thine heart was lifted up because of thy beauty, thou hast corrupted thy wisdom by reason of thy brightness: I will cast thee to the ground, I will lay thee before kings, that they may behold thee.

This is the account of the righteous judgment of God to Lucifer. He was adequately dealt with. When he sinned, God drove him away from his presence in disgrace. His wisdom was corrupted, and his personality changed, then he became the devil/Satan, and all angels under him became demons because they supported his aspiration. As a result of his fall and his violent response to the judgment of God, the earth, his abode, was destroyed and became a chaotic mass. I believe it was the devil that destroyed the earth and then lived in the atmosphere because God wouldn't have destroyed the beautiful earth he created in his majesty. The devil would have destroyed the earth in a bid to prevent God from creating another creature to occupy the earth.

The judgment of the devil and the destruction of the earth are what resulted to what we read in Genesis 1:2, "Now the earth was formless and empty, darkness was over the surface of the deep." Jeremiah 4:23-24 says, "I looked at the earth and it was formless and empty, and their light was gone. I looked at mountains, and they were swaying." The above scriptures show that the earth had light and mountains during the pre-Adamic kingdom, but they could not be found in Genesis 1:2 because the earth had become a chaotic mass. The earth became formless and empty; there was nothing useful on the earth. The entire earth was covered with water, and the lights were no more there. "Now the earth formless and empty, darkness was over the surface of the deep" (Gen. 1:2).

The Hebrew word for *now* in the above scripture is *attah*, which means "at this time or henceforth." This suggests that the earth used to be perfectly intact before the sudden and violent chaos that fell on the earth. The best word, *attah* can also mean "an instantaneous change of a particular scenario." It can also be expressed as God saying, "At this time [now], the earth was formless." The Hebrew word for *formless* is *tohuw*, and it means *desolate*. The perfect earth became desolate, which suggests the destruction of the perfect and beautiful earth. "At this time, the [perfect] earth was desolate and empty."

The Hebrew word for *empty* is *bohuw*, which means *void*, an indistinguishable ruin. This tells us that the desolation of the earth was so terrible that its ruin was heartbreaking to God; in other words, "at this time [now], the [perfect] earth was desolate and became an indistinguishable ruin. Darkness . . ." The Hebrew word for *darkness* here is *choshek*, which means "misery, destruction, or wickedness." It talks about the disorder of something that used to be good. The scripture can then be rendered as "at this time [now], the [perfect] earth was a desolate and indistinguishable ruin. Disorderliness [darkness] was over the surface of the deep."

When Lucifer fell and became Satan, everything on the earth went wrong; the earth was desolate and an indistinguishable ruin. Satan and his demons could not stay on the earth any longer because of the condition of the earth; they therefore relocated to the high places in the second heaven, but they could not enter the third heaven.

CHAPTER THREE

THE ADAMIC KINGDOM

AFTER THE DESOLATION of the pre-Adamic kingdom, re-creation of the desolated earth took place; the Holy Spirit had to do the work of incubation first before the creation was spoken into manifestation. The Bible says, "And the earth was without form, and void; and darkness was upon the face of the deep. And the Spirit of God moved upon the face of the waters" (Gen. 1:2).

The New International Version of the above scripture states thus: "Now the earth was formless and empty, darkness was over the surface of the deep, and the Spirit of God was hovering over the waters" (Gen. 1:2). What that means is that the Spirit of God was incubating the chaotic earth. The Hebrew word for *hovering* is *rachaph*, which means "brood, flutter, move, or shake." The Holy Spirit incubated the chaotic earth. There was something he shook together in a manner of incubation to make the earth ready for the Word of God for re-creation. This is a creative ability of God at work; this is the same power God gave to the new creation.

The created earth had become a soup of nothingness, a bottomless emptiness, and an inky blackness. But later, God's Spirit brooded like a bird above the watery abyss. After proper and successful incubation, a voice came out of heaven in verse 3

of Genesis's chapter 1: "And God said 'Let there be light, and there
was light.'" God spoke light into creation first as a preparation for
the re-creation of the chaotic world because God would not work
in the dark. God said, "Let there be light"; the Hebrew word for
light here is *owr*, which means *illumination*. God illuminated the
earth in order to have brightness and send darkness away. This is
a lesson for us since we have the very creative ability of God; we
should learn to create light first before creating any other thing.
The Word is our light; if you can dwell and meditate on the
Word of God, the light will come, then you can do anything
with the ability of God in you. The created light is the morning
or sun. Invariably, God created light first to illuminate the earth.
He spoke the light into being authoritatively. Creation is done by
divine authority.

If you want to create anything as a Christian, you have
to do it authoritatively. What God actually said is *"Light be!"*
when he created light in his spoken Word; thus, we are required
to speak into manifestation with our mouths (in the name of
Jesus) whatever we want to see after brooding on the matter by
meditation on the Word and supremacy of God with the power
of the Holy Ghost. As a new creation, we brood on a matter by
meditation and envision that thing with hours of the spirit.

God separated the light from the darkness. "God called
the light day. And the darkness he called night. And there was
evening, and there was morning, the first day" (Gen. 1:5). God
sustained the light by the power of his word and totally eradicated
darkness from day. He separated the light from the darkness in
order to make room for the existence of day and night, morning
and evening, for the accountability of days, weeks, months, and
years for proper documentation.

God proceeded to separate water from water. "And God said,
Let there be a firmament in the midst of the waters, and let it
divide the waters from the waters. And God made the firmament,
and divided the waters which were under the firmament from the
waters which were above the firmament: and it was so. And God
called the firmament Heaven. And the evening and the morning

were the second day" (Gen. 1:6-8). "As a result of the destruction of the hearth, Water covered the whole earth to the first heaven. God made separation between the first heaven and earth by the separation of the water that covered everything and the first heaven was called sky. And it was so God called the dry ground land and gathered waters He called seas" (Gen. 1:9-10). The gathered waters obeyed God's voice by giving chance for the manifestation of dry ground for the progressive work of re-creation. This is the reason the Bible declares that God founded the earth upon the seas and established it upon the waters in Psalm 24:4.

Since land had been made available, "then God said, let the land produce vegetation seed bearing plants and trees on the land that bear fruit with seed in it, according to their various kind. And God saw that it was good" (Gen. 1:11-12) God proceeded to speak the light in the expanse of the sky into existence in order to separate the day from the night to serve as signs to identify seasons, days, and years. In verse 5 of Genesis's chapter 1, God spoke a light to existence; that is the very light he was still talking about in verse 14.

What God was doing in particular was the allocation of the sun to where it was supposed to be and was separating the work of that illumination into the sun and moon. It must be added that God did create the moon. He created *owr*, the sun. It is the rotation of the sun that enables the moon for the purpose of having days and nights. You'll notice that in Genesis 1:3, "And God said, 'let there be lights.'" The word *lights* is pluralized, and the Hebrew word is *maowr*, which talks about the plurality of the *owr*'s influence. God made the sun to be the greater light and called it day; it is the greater light that gives to the lesser light to reflect of its glory and to be a light for the night. "The greater light was assigned to govern the day and the lesser light to govern the night." After this, God made stars (Gen. 1:14-16).

God ordered the water on the earth to teem with living creatures and birds to fly above and across the expanse of the earth in Genesis 1:20. He spoke to the dry ground called land to produce living creatures according to their kinds: livestock, creatures that move along the ground, and wild animals—each according to their kinds. After speaking all of them into creation, he said they were good, which means the re-created earth was perfect.

THE CREATION OF MAN

The perfect earth was without any manager, and then God decided to create a manager or a caretaker. Before the creation of the caretaker, Satan, the fallen archangel, could have probably been somewhere, looking at the re-created work, expecting to know what God was about to do. To his amazement, "God said, let us make man in our image, in our likeness and let them rule over the livestock, over all the earth, and over all the creatures that move along the ground" (Gen. 1:26).

God pronounced his primary plan. His declaration about man's creation was made clear. The existence of every other creature was made without any existing thing or likeness of any creature, but man's existence was from two dimensions: man was made and created. God said, "Let us make." The Hebrew word *asah* was chosen, and it means "to make, to accomplish." He said, "In our image." The Hebrew word for *image* is *tselem*, which means "to shade" or "a phantom." It can also be said to mean "a resemblance or a statue." The mind of God was to make a shade or, better still, a house to accommodate man; man himself is referred to as a phantom—a ghost or, better still, a spirit. Thus, what God made with dust is not the real man but his shade—his house to relate with the physical world.

The body is the shade or house where the real man would live. When the Bible says that God made man in his image, it's talking about God creating or building a house where the human spirit would live that looks exactly like God. In view of that, it's established that the body of man was made like a statue that looks exactly like God to shade the real man who is a phantom—a spirit.

Genesis 2:7 explains the process by which the building of the house (statue) that shades man was built: "And the Lord

God formed man." The Hebrew word for *formed* is *yatsar*, which means "to make by squeezing into shape" or "to mold into a form like a potter." It actually talks about squeezing into shape out of already existing material—from the dust of the ground. The remaining part of the discussed in Genesis 1:26 says, "In our likeness." The Hebrew word is *demuwth*, which means "resemblance in manner." God formed the body of man in his image in a structure that looks exactly like him. He prepared a shade that looks exactly like him for the man and also made him a spirit being that also resembles him in character. God created man to resemble him in appearance and attitude. When God said, "Let us make man in our image in our likeness," the word *likeness* is talking about the making of the soul of man because the soul of man comprises mind, heart, and will, and they are what determine the character of a man.

Genesis 2:7, "The Lord God formed the man from the dust of the ground and breathed into his nostrils the breath of life and the man became a living being." Having formed the statue, shade, or house that looked like God, God breathed into the nostrils of the statue the breath of life. The breath of life that God breathed into the statue was not the Spirit of God. The fact is that man had already been created at the time; he was first created, but he existed in the realm of the spirit conceptually. He could not be seen because he had no physical house to relate to the physical world, and nothing was said about him because his process of creation to live on earth was not yet completed, but he existed in God. Since God is spirit and man is spirit, it was easy for man to live in God just as God lives in us (the Christians) today. So man existed in God before the body was made to house him.

Genesis 1:27, "So God created man in his own image, in the image of God he Created him; male and female he created them." The word *create* is *bara* in the Hebrew language; it is the complete package of the spirit and the formed statue that looks and acts like God. This happened when God breathed the breath of life into the nostrils of the body, and immediately the man became a living being or a living soul. The Hebrew word for *soul* is *nephesh*, which means "breath, thought, and emotions." *Nephesh* is the very likeness of God.

So God created us to think, act, and have his own kind of emotion. To think like God tells us that we can reason like God, and to have his kind of emotion shows that man is supposed to love and act like God. The likeness of God in man is more spiritual than physical. It is the divinity residing in humanity. Man was initially not created to be inferior or subject to any other creature until the fall of Adam.

The likeness of God in man is what makes man greater than all other living creatures because God gave his likeness to man only, and that is why God could entrust the whole world to man's care. God said, "And let them rule . . . over all earth" (Gen. 1:26).

Man is a spirit; he has a soul and lives in a body. It is through a body that man contacts with the material world. The body is what gives man world consciousness because that is the mechanism by which human beings relate to the physical world. The soul of man comprises the intellect that helps man in the state of emotions that are processed from senses. The soul belongs to man's own self and reveals his/her personality. It is the part of self-consciousness.

The spirit of man is the man himself; the spirit of man communes with God. It is the medium by which man is able to worship God. The spirit of man is the element of God consciousness. God dwells in the spirit; the self dwells in the soul while senses dwell in the body. By the spirit, man relates with the spiritual world; this is the ability to receive and express the power and life of God from the spirit realm. When a man is born again, it is the spirit that is born of God. It takes conscious effort of the new creation to renew his mind with the Word of God. The man's soul functions with the aid of the information that was stored in it by observation and/or experience; that is why the new creation must program his mind with the Word of God to be able to accurately function like God.

Through the body, man relates to the sensuous world. The soul of man stands between the man's spirit and his body yet belongs to both of them because the human soul is the link between the spiritual and physical world. The human soul stands between the human spirit and body, binding the two together. The spirit can subdue the body through the medium of a soul so the body will obey God. Likewise, the body can subdue the mind and influence the spirit. Thus, you have to let your spirit rule your soul to subdue your body. If you must live the glorious life in the body of Christ, you must renew your mind with the Word of God to allow your spirit to dominate both soul and body. The reason many Christians live dirty lives is because they were unable to allow their spirits to subdue their bodies through the medium of souls to obey the will of God.

THE LIVING SOUL

This is what makes man become a living being; man can also be called a living soul because it is in the soul that the heat of life is located, and the working of the heart is what makes man to be a living soul because blood is generated from the heart and as it is stated in the scripture that blood is the life of the body; thus, man is a living soul.

Remember, whenever a man has heart failure, it always leads to death. In fact, any heart problem is regarded as a very critical problem because that is the zone and power of life. Any heart failure actually means a disconnection of the spirit from the body, which equals to physical death.

The heart also functions emotionally; any information received by the mind and has some emotional ingredient would definitely produce real natures of emotion in the heart (either love or hatred). Man cannot love or hate without the mind receiving information, thinking it through, deliberating on it, and sending it to the heart. Originally, man cannot love without his mind because it is the mind that will make all the necessary arrangements for the heart to manifest love or hatred emotionally.

The ability to receive information with the mind is of God's likeness because God has a mind that he receives information with. God also has a heart, which he feels emotionally with; this is the reason he could love us and hate sin. God also has a component—will; that is why God can make decisions.

In all these, we can deduce that it is only man out of all creatures that God gave his likeness; that is why man's creation is obviously different from any other creature, and this is what makes man a unique being.

The mind of man is the epicenter of man's personality with which one receives information. It is the door to the human spirit and body. Information received with the mind dictates the immediate and future reactions of the human spirit and his body. Whenever men come across any information in a book or somewhere else, it is the mind that does the job of thinking on the information. It is the mind of man that records events and processes them. Anything man sees, hears, tastes, feels, and touches goes straight to the mind to make an interpretation, to create a recording, and to send it to the heart.

Thinking capacity is in the mind; it is the mind that does the thinking. The mind possesses the power of imagination, and that is where man's intellect is located. The target of Satan against people is their minds. Second Corinthians 4:4 says, "The god of this age has blinded the minds of unbelievers." That is why Romans 12:2 warns, "Do not conform any longer to the patterns of this world, but be transformed by the renewing of your mind."

As a Christian, the onus to guide your mind from not being colonized by the devil and living dirtily is in your mind. God will not guide your mind for you. Thus, it is so important for you to dwell in the Word of God and program your mind according to the will of God for your life.

The heart of man is one of the three components of the soul. It is an organ in man's chest. The heart is referred to as the center of life, "for the life of a creature is in the blood" (Lev. 17:11). This is what makes man a living creature. Man is called a living soul because the heart is part of the soul.

The heart is also a tool for emotions; any information that the mind receives and has some emotional element will be made manifest in the heart. The emotion may be love, hatred, joy, or sorrow. You cannot love or hate without receiving the information in the mind. The mind and heart work hand in hand. The mind relies on senses, and the heart relies on the mind to get information to function with.

Will is another major component of the soul; it is the part of a human soul's component that does the final manifestation of any information. The will is in the attitude of man by which a person makes a decision and takes action. Whatever the mind receives, thinks about, deliberates on, and sends to the heart is what will be sent to the last component—the will—for the decision making that determines a man's action. God made man to be a living soul so man will be able to make decisions and be responsible for his actions. The power of decision making is in the will. Your will determines what you want to do and how to do it. This is where the initial freedom of man starts from because it gives man the enablement to choose either right or wrong. God made man to be a free moral agent by giving him a soul.

However, the ability to receive information with the mind is the likeness of God because God has a mind with which he receives information. God also has a heart with which he feels emotions; this is the reason he can love us and hate sin. God also has will; that is why he can make decisions and execute them.

Thus, you are a free moral agent. God or the devil will not make decisions for you. What God or the devil can do is to talk, guide, motivate, or influence you to make a decision based on the information available at your disposal, and the information at your disposal is determined by the environment you have, the education you have, the kind of books you read, the kind of movies you watch, the music you listen to, etc.

This is the reason God cannot force anybody to accept Christ though Jesus died for the whole world because God loves all human creatures and doesn't want anyone to perish, but the decision to accept Christ lies on every individual, not on God. The only thing God can do is to guide them to receive the Word of God to change their minds to accept Christ, and he can send people to preach the Word of God to them, but the onus of accepting Christ is still on them, not on God.

The same thing is applicable when it comes to the issue of faith and receiving from God. Though God is love and doesn't want us to lack anything, it takes our faith to receive from God and possess our possessions as a new creation, but we have to program our minds with the Word of God to work in faith, receive from God, and possess our possessions.

However, it is important to know the importance of faith in the Christian work because "without faith it is impossible to please God, because anyone who comes to him must believe that he exists and that he rewards those who earnestly seek him" (Heb. 11:6).

THE PERFECT EARTH

We have seen how beautiful earth was initially created and how exceptional man was created. All the beautiful things had been put in place; everything needed had been made available. And man was created in the image and likeness of God to have dominion over the beautiful world as well as enjoy great freedom.

Proper arrangement of the earth was done; all creatures were put where God wanted them to be. All animals lived with Adam in harmony. The beauty of the Garden of Eden was at the extreme; its beauty was highly enviable. Adam lived in the garden in full harmonious enjoyment and had a close relationship with God Almighty; it was a unique experience for Adam in the cool of the day. God used to talk to him, and he also talked to God amicably. He had a close and amicable communication with God.

They were friends according to their relationship; God loved him so much and committed many things to his care. All these were made possible because God had created man in his own image and his likeness. God could intimately interact with man not only because man was created in the image of God from the dust of the ground but particularly because man was created in the very likeness of God with the proper function of a soul: mind, heart, and will. For instance, the Bible says, "Now the Lord God had formed out of the ground all the beast of the field and all the birds of the air. He brought them to the man to see what he would name them, and whatever the man called each living creature, that was its names. So that man gave names to all the livestock, the birds of the air all the beasts of the field" (Gen. 2:19-20).

God entrusted the naming of all creatures to the man's care because he had the mind, heart, and will to do the work suitably. God allowed Adam to name all the creatures because he had created him with a creative ability; thus he decided what their names should be respectively. This could be done like God by his creative ability. God created Adam to be greater than any other creature, including Satan. This is what provoked Satan against man with passion. Satan could not help the situation because man was created by God for a special purpose: to subdue the earth and rule over everything that exists, including the devil.

THEN CAME A WOMAN

When God created man (Adam), he did not create him with an angelic nature and not even with God's nature. Man was created with a special and perfect (Adamic) nature. The Adamic nature was a very special nature. God made this nature to be an exceptional nature and free of domination by external forces. God did not leave man all alone in discharging his responsibility, but he stood with him and communed with him every day. As a matter of fact, God must have been teaching him basic things because he is the teacher of life; therefore, I know God would have been teaching Adam different things about life and his godliness whenever they met in the cool of the day because man requires teaching in order to develop his mind to maturity.

Because God always thought about the well-being of the man, he always wanted him to live in perfect peace, without lacking any good thing. God looked at all the things around Adam. He noticed man was lacking a suitable helper, then he made all the beasts of the fields and all the birds of the air, including all the fishes, but none of these creatures qualified to be a suitable helper for Adam.

Therefore, God caused Adam to fall into a deep sleep, and while he was still sleeping, God took one of Adam's ribs and closed up the place with flesh. Then God made a woman from the rib he had taken out of the man, and he brought her to him for his assessment (see Gen. 2:20-24).

God therefore created a beautiful woman out of the man; she was another type of man that would be an intimate companion for the man and a coworker to fulfill the assignment given to the man by God. We can see that all that God created was very good, but when God discovered the exclusion of woman in man's life, God saw that something was going wrong. God declared that "it is not good for the man to be alone" (Gen. 2:18). It was when God created woman that everything became perfectly good. That was where companionship and partnership started from. That is where God's dream of reproduction started its fulfillment.

EVE AND THE SERPENT

Immediately after the creation of the woman, everything became very good. The man discovered the task before him was achievable now; he discovered that he was having a perfect partner. He automatically recognized who she was; that is why he said, "This is now bone of my bones and flesh of my flesh; she shall be called woman for she was taken out of man" (Gen. 2:23). Adam caught the vision; immediately he set his eye on the new creature. Adam recognized the fact that the newly created fellow was taken from his bone.

The man and the woman continued their lives together as husband and wife. God entrusted man with the responsibility of orientating the woman. God expected the man to teach the woman all that he had taught him. The woman had to know the instructions and love of God by paying attention to the man.

Adam actually told Eve all that God told him according to the will of God. But there was something that requires our attentions elsewhere.

When Eve was communicating with Satan, she said, "But God did say 'you must not eat fruit from the tree that is in the middle of the garden, and you must not touch it or you will die'" (Gen. 3:3). Compare this with Genesis 2:17 when God said, "But you must not eat from the tree of the knowledge of good and evil, for when you eat of it you will surely die." The information in Genesis 2:17 is the real instruction that God gave to Adam, but when Eve quoted the words in Genesis 3:3, she added, "You must not touch it." God did not tell Adam not to touch the tree; after all, God told Adam to dress the garden, and it would not have been possible for them to clean the garden perfectly without touching a particular tree in the middle of the garden. However, the tree of the knowledge of good and evil was in the middle of the garden; definitely, that place required more immaculate attention.

I wonder where Eve got her information, but I believe the added information was not originally from God. It is an exaggeration either from Adam when he was teaching Eve or from Eve herself.

Actually, Satan hated man because of how God created man and gave him dominion. Satan hated God, man, and the dream of reproduction. Satan was more furious when he saw God creating the woman because he knew the fulfillment of the reproduction was glaringly getting to fulfillment stage, knowing fully the consequence of the fulfillment of reproduction to him and his demons. Satan knows that man will judge him and his demons; for this reason, he would do anything to make man fall and be subject to him. Satan knows very well the quality, authority, and power that accompanies the nature of man.

The Adamic nature is a consecrated nature with created divine power. So Satan envied the man because of his nature, and he systematically strategized the way to steal his authority and corrupt his nature because he had corrupted his own angelic nature. Satan made a clear-cut plan: he knew mankind could be attacked from the point of their exaggeration, and he decided to plan the fall of man through that medium.

THE ENTRANCE OF SIN

On that terrible and historical day, Satan entered the Garden of Eden in the appearance of the craftiest animal—the serpent. Satan did this because he could not enter like an angel. When he entered, he said to the woman, "Did God really say you must not eat from any tree in the garden?" (Gen. 3:1).

Satan knew God did not say they should not eat from any of the trees in the garden, but he used this as his set induction to the temptation. We must remember Satan had strategized perfectly before he came inside the garden with his plans; Satan really meant business and determined to win the conversation.

This is a good lesson; we must be very careful with the way we attend to our thoughts because our thinking faculty is the medium that Satan always targets whenever he wants to tempt us. We can deduce from Satan's conversation with the woman that he did not ask her to eat the fruit of the tree of knowledge of good and evil in the first place, but he focused her attention on the fruit of the tree via the conversation and gave an impression of giving her an information that would benefit her. Satan presented his statement to accuse God falsely, and the woman stood her ground to defend God at the initial place. She replied to Satan's diplomatic question exaggeratedly; she said, "We may eat but fruit from the tree that in the middle of the garden, and you must not touch it, or you will die" (Gen. 3:23). What a brilliant reply but very exaggerated.

Satan used that added clause to take advantage of the woman. Satan drew the woman's attention to the tree strongly. Satan might have probably sat on the tree in order to draw the woman's attention to some fresh fruits on the tree. He told her that nothing bad would happen if she touched or ate the fruit from this tree of knowledge of good and evil; instead, they would be independent of God. They would be as powerful as God. More so, they must have been dressing the tree of good and evil and necessarily touched it because God instructed them to dress the entire Garden of Eden; therefore, this could have made the woman to come near the tree and touched it while nothing happened.

This will necessarily give Satan a very easy avenue to prove Eve's statement wrong and manipulated her to eat the fruit of the tree for if nothing happened to her when she touched the tree, then nothing would happen to her if she ate the fruit of the tree. After the woman's attention had been drawn to the tree, Satan then said to the woman, "You will not surely die, 'the serpent said to the woman, for God knows that when you eat of it your eyes will be opened, and you will be like God knowing good and evil'" (Gen. 3:4-5). Satan assured the woman that she would not die, convincing her with many lies by using the woman's exaggeration as a tool. I believe the transaction between Satan and the woman lasted some long period of time because the conversation probably involved some arguments, but the well-prepared Satan would not give up.

We have to recognize the fact that when Satan wants you to do something, he will not fight with you, but he will pet you and speak some sweet words with diplomatic lies that can make anybody do his will if care is not taken. Satan knows that human nature loves good things; he therefore told the woman that God knew that the fruits of this tree had the ability to open their eyes and their cognitive domains and would improve and enhance their personal decision making. Satan lied to the woman that the fruit of the tree had the ability to make them to be like God because he knew that if man thought and dared to be like God, God would be upset and break the relationship. The continuation of this evil conversation actually made them fall to the devil; thus, man became the enemy of God. Remember, this is the kind of sin that Satan committed against God—high treason.

Eve had never heard this kind of false mystery before; she therefore made a trial after critical thought over the issue. She took a close look at the fruit of the tree. The Bible declares, "And when the woman saw that the tree was good for food, and that it was pleasant to the eyes, and a tree to be desired to make one wise, she took of the fruit thereof, and did eat, and gave also unto her husband with her; and he did eat" (Gen. 3:6). This scripture has been severely misreported by many folks. Many people claimed that Adam was not around when the woman ate the fruit; they said Adam went to the farm and the woman kept the fruit for him to eat.

But the real biblical report is that Adam was with Eve during the discussion with Satan. He definitely heard their conversation; he knew what they were talking about, but he could not demonstrate what he possessed as a man of authority to stop the conversation. I am still puzzled on why Adam left them and was influenced.

Immediately when they ate the fruit of the tree, they died spiritually. Death came to their immortal bodies. Their relationship with God was cut off. An end was pronounced to their amicable relationship with God. They could not commune with God any longer. Sin entered their lives, and they became sinners. The Adamic authority was stolen by Satan. Satan conquered them diplomatically. They could not help the matter; they were relegated to the background. Iniquity set into the world and dominated the human creature. They became the slaves of the devil. They could not function in the realm of the spirit. They were subjected to their flesh and sensory knowledge.

Originally, they functioned in the spirit and put their body and soul to work in subject to the will of God, but when they ate the fruit of the tree, their spiritual eyes could not see again because they were spiritually dead. Alternatively, their physical eyes opened (see Gen. 3:7). The natural view took over their lives, and sensory knowledge dominated them. They could do nothing in the spirit realm. They considered nothing from the spiritual point of view. The most unfortunate part of the case is that physical eyes cannot see anything good; physical eyes see only trouble, condemnation, and failure. For instance, the very first thing Adam and Eve saw was their nakedness, and they immediately felt condemned. They did not stop there; they went ahead to provide a personal solution to their problem by sewing fig leaves together and made coverings for themselves (Gen. 3:7).

They believed they could get things done out without God's agency. From that moment, the human race dwelt in condemnation, chaos, and trouble, and calamitous failure became a major feature of the human race because of the fall of Adam and Eve in the Garden of Eden. The entire human race was cursed, and all mankind became sinners. The satanic nature set in and dominated the entire human race.

Man stopped functioning with the Adamic nature because Adam lost it in the garden. From that moment of sin till now, no human lived and/or functioned with the Adamic nature but with the satanic nature until Jesus came, died, and resurrected. It is only we that are born again that had put off the satanic nature and put on the divine nature of God (ZOE). Make no mistake about it: no man has the Adamic nature even now; better still, there is no man with the proper human nature. No man will live with the proper human nature because it was corrupted when Adam sinned in the Garden of Eden. Every Christian has the nature of God; it is the divine nature—eternal life (ZOE) that will live and function while every man that is not born again has the satanic nature.

THE HEAVENS

Genesis 1:1 reads, "In the beginning God created the HEAVENS." God created more than one heaven. He created three heavens. Many people think he created one heaven and dwelt there. Some people say that God created seven heavens, but the truth is that he created three heavens.

The heavens are part of the major components of the universe; God set the sun, the moon, and the stars in one of the heavens. God dwells in the third heaven, and that is where Christ is and where we have our names registered as Zionists. We will dwell in the third heaven with Christ when we rapture; the Christians who have died are already there now.

Second Corinthians 12:2 and 4 talks about the third heaven, and it was made known that the place is the paradise. You don't have to be told again that the fact that there is a third heaven shows that there are a first and second heaven and that the third heaven is the highest heaven because 2 Corinthians 12:2 and 4 shows that the third heaven is paradise (where God dwells).

The first heaven is right above the earth; it is called the atmospheric heaven or the lower heaven. The second heaven is right above the first heaven. It is out in space. It is the region where the stars, moon, sun, and planets are; it is called the stellar heaven or space. When God said "Let there be light," that is where he focused his attention, and there was light. There are two great lights in the second heaven to mark the seasons, days, and years. He also made stars in there. The second heaven is the middle heaven or the firmament.

The third heaven is where God Almighty dwells in his glory. The third heaven is the paradise. That is where Jesus sits in power at the right hand of God. "After the Lord Jesus had spoken to them, he was taken up into heaven and he sat at the right hand of God" (Mark 16:19). Jesus defeated the devil and sat at the right hand of majesty in heaven (Heb. 1:3). He sits at the seat of power in heaven. This is one of what guarantees our authority as believers in this present earth. Every Christian is a member of the household of God located in the third heaven because we are the citizens of heaven. You are no longer foreigners and aliens but fellow citizens with God's people and members of God's household (Eph. 2:19). What this means is that you are a citizen of the third heaven if you are born again. That is why the Bible says, "But our citizenship is in heaven" (Phil. 3:20).

Having understood the origin of Lucifer, his sin, and his fall, we deduced that he lived on the earth even with the understanding of three heavens. We must add at this point that the earth is part of the universe; it is the particle world. Thus, the inhabitants of the earth, even Lucifer, must have a physical body with which they can relate to the earth.

We studied that Lucifer was created of stones just like man was created from the dust of the ground. The same Hebrew word *bara*, which talks about a formative process and was used for the creation of man, was used in Ezekiel 28:13 to describe the creation of Lucifer; moreover, we all know that angels are spirit beings, including Lucifer, but Lucifer needed a physical body to be able to live on the earth. This is the reason his body was created from physical stones.

We are not of the world and do not belong to the first or second heaven. Our citizenship is in heaven. Our place is in heaven; we are here on the earth to preach the gospel and bring people to the knowledge of the Word of God. We have a mandate to reconcile the unsaved ones to God and to let them know the sacrifice Jesus made for us.

THE FLOOD

During the dispensation of conscience, the satanic nature deeply influenced the living beings on the planet earth. The Bible tells us that at that time, men began to increase in number on the planet earth. The dream of God to populate the earth was fulfilling, and I am convinced that God would have been happy about this. But the satanic influence, wickedness and selfishness, increased greatly.

The greatest satanic influence that really caught the attention of God is reported in verse 2 of chapter 6 of the book of Genesis that says, "The sons of God saw that the daughters of men were beautiful, and they married any of them they chose." This is one of the scriptures that have also been misinterpreted by many Christians. Some folks said that the phrase "The sons of God" is talking about some set of people on the earth that chose to be his people, but this is not true. The word *sons* in that sentence is talking about the fallen angels; this will be properly elucidated by the Word of God in order to avoid heresy.

THE SONS OF GOD

The phrase "sons of God" refers to fallen angels. In the book of Jude 1:6, the Bible declares, "And the angels who did not keep their position of authority but abandoned their own home—these he has kept in darkness, bound with ever lasting chains for judgment of the great day." This is pointing to a situation where some of these angels refused to maintain their angelic jurisdictions. The Bible also made mention of "their own home" in the above verse. This is to tell us that those angels apparently were assigned specific locations as well as responsibilities; as a matter of fact, these angels fell with Lucifer. They manipulated and made man to fall. And after the fall of man, they easily communicated with men and intermarried with their daughters. Though they were not bodily beings, they were able to get human bodies to be able to relate with the physical world.

> "The sons of God saw that the daughters of men were beautiful, and they married any of them they choose" (Gen. 6:12).

> "And GOD saw that the wickedness of man was great in the earth, and that every imagination of the thoughts of his heart was only evil continually" (Gen. 6:5).

> "The earth also was corrupt before God, and the earth was filled with violence" (Gen. 6:11).

Proper evaluation of these verses will help to understand what the phrase "the sons of God" does not mean, which will help us to understand what it means.

In verse 5 of chapter 6 of the book of Genesis, we read that God saw that man was too wicked and sinful. God actually referred to all the human creatures on the surface of earth, excluding Noah who found favor in the sight of God. During this period, there was no man that was qualified to be called the son of God on earth. They all had the nature of the devil. There was no way they would please God because their minds were their governors and subject to the devil.

Moreover, Noah was not the "son" of God—neither were his male children. During this period, every man on earth functioned in the total manifestation of the satanic nature. Noah and his household were only favored by God for the purpose of protecting the plan of God and extending the human generation on the face of the earth till the time of Jesus. Therefore, no human person could be referred to as a son of God or a set of people be called the sons of God.

In verse 11 of chapter 6 of the book of Genesis, it was also made clear that the earth was corrupt in God's sight and was full of violence. If God was having any human beings as his sons on the earth, he would have discussed more about them. But the fallen angels were referred to as the sons of God because they (angels) were spiritual beings that used to function in heaven before they lost their places because of Satan's high treason.

By now, it should be clear to us that the phrase "the sons of God" is referring to the fallen angels. It must be noted that the intermarriages in this verse were intermarriages and cohabitations between divine and human beings. And the intermarriage between divine and human beings violated the order of creation. This violation of the order of creation grieved God, and he immediately pronounced that "my spirits will not contend with man forever, for he is mortal, his days will be a hundred and twenty years" (Gen. 6:3). Man had become mortal, subject to death even though he was originally created to be immortal in the very beginning. Man became mortal because the satanic nature produced death; that is why God told Adam in the first place that "but you must not eat from the tree of the knowledge of good and evil, for when you eat of it you will surely die" (Gen. 2:17).

God was talking about spiritual death here; the spiritual death is what makes man mortal and ensures the physical death. Physical death is not possible without the spiritual death first because man is a spirit.

The intermarriages and cohabitations between the fallen angels and daughters of men led to the birth of the Nephilim. The Nephilim were of great size and strength. There is a particular size for man, but the children from the intermarriages between the fallen angels and the human beings were big or gigantic—big in size and full of supernatural strength.

Nephilim is the Hebrew word for "fallen ones." Nephilim does not mean "fallen angels" but "fallen ones." This is because they are the product of the fallen angels and sinful men. The Nephilim were people of great size and divine strength—big and giant in human senses, but in God's eyes, they were sinners and fallen ones that must be wiped out of the earth. They were men with six toes.

For the first time, God was grieved and regretted that he had made man on the face of the earth, and his heart was filled with pain (Gen. 6:6). "And the LORD said, I will destroy man whom I have created from the face of the earth; both man, and beast, and the creeping thing, and the fowls of the air; for it repenteth me that I have made them" (Gen. 6:7). The growth and radiation of sin and the great weakness of mankind grew; therefore, they must be wiped out of the face of the earth—not only mankind but also the animals and every other creature that moved along the ground and also the birds of the air. God did not want anything to remain without being wiped out of the earth because they had no connection with God.

But God was still having his original purpose of replenishing the earth in mind. He deliberately set Noah and his household aside and favored them because they obeyed him. God resumed his plan with Noah and his household for the purpose of replenishing the earth. As a matter of fact, nobody qualified to be called righteous, but Noah had been favored by God and set aside as a vessel unto honor that would be used to fulfill God's purpose on the earth. The Bible says, "But Noah found favor in the eyes of the Lord" (Gen. 6:8). The Bible declared Noah as a righteous man, blameless among the people of his time and walking with God (see Gen. 6:9). the above verse made it declared that Noah actually found favor in the eyes of the Lord. This is an active grace of God at work even in the midst of his plan of judgment. God still singled Noah and his household out to be favored. God chose Noah as a vessel and instrument to carry out his judgment on earth. God called Noah and told him his original plan was not to put an end to the existence of the living beings on earth though the earth was filled with sin and violence. But God was determined to wipe away sin and its agents. God therefore chose Noah to sustain the original plan of God for the earth and mankind. God instructed Noah to make an ark of cypress wood for himself and his people. He should make rooms in it and coat it with pitch inside and out (see Gen. 6:13-14).

God told Noah to build the ark of cypress wood like this: the ark was to be 450 feet long, 75 feet wide, and 45 feet high. God said he should make a roof for the ark and finish the ark to be within eighteen inches at the top. God said Noah should put a door on the sides of the ark and make lower, middle, and upper decks (Gen. 6:15-16).

After all these were done, God established his covenant with Noah. Noah entered the ark with his three sons, his wife, and his son's wives. Noah brought in with himself two of all living creatures (a male and female)—two of every kind of creature that moved along the ground. Noah took every kind of food that was to be eaten and stored them. All these he did according to God's instructions (see Gen. 6:18-22). After Noah had done what God instructed him to do, then God shut them inside the ark (see Gen. 7:16).

After this, it started raining. The rain became a flood. The flood kept coming onto the earth, and as the waters increased, they were lifted high above the earth (see Gen. 17:17). This terrible flood (of judgment) lasted for a hundred and fifty days; the water later dried up, and God asked Noah to come out of the ark with those in the ark. After he had come out of the ark, he built an altar to the Lord and took some of all the clean animals and clean birds; he sacrificed burned offerings on the altar to worship God. The Lord smelled the pleasing aroma and said in his heart, "Never again will I destroy all living creatures, as I have done" (see Gen. 8:20-21).

Noah continued living on the face of the earth with his household; these are the ones that reproduced and made the purpose of God continue. The sons of Noah were Shem, Ham, and Japheth.

These sons had children after the flood; they were the ones that populated the earth, and I would like to discuss them briefly in a respective manner.

THE SEMITES

Shem was the elder brother of Japheth, and he was the ancestor of all the sons of Eber. The descendants of Shem were called Shemites (later modified to Semites). Shem gave birth to Elam, Asshir, Arphaxed, Lud, and Aram.

The descendants of Elam were called the Elamites; they lived in the east of Mesopotamia. Asshur was called Assyria in southern Mesopotamia, not really far from the Garden of Eden. Arphaxed's descendants lived in southern Mesopotamia. Lud's descendants were known as the Ludites and were the Lydians of Asia Minor. Aram's descendants were located at the northeast of Canaan. This is the area called Syria today (see Gen. 10:21-25).

Ham had four sons: Cush, Mizraim, Put, and Canaan. His descendants are called Hamites; Hamites were located in Southwestern Asia and Northeast Africa. Cush, one of Ham's sons, lived at the upper Nile region south of Egypt. Mizraim could be traced down to both upper and lower Egypt. Put is deduced to be the ancient Egyptians called Punt in the modern Somalia, and other information referred to them in Libya. Canaan—this is referred to as the land of purple. Canaan was the major producer and exporter of purple dye. The land was later called today's Palestine after the Philistines (see Gen. 10:6).

THE JAPHETHITES

Japheth was the oldest son of Noah. He gave birth to seven sons. They are Gomer, Magog, Madai, Javan, Tubal, Meshech, and Tiras. The Japhethites lived in Eurasia in the north and west of Palestine. Gomer's descendants lived near the Black Sea. Magog was traced down to possibly be the father of a Scythian people who inhabited Caucasia and adjacent regions southeast of the Black Sea. Madai's descendants were later called Medes. Javan lived at southern Greece. Tubal lived in Pointus, and Meshech lived in the Moschian Mountains. Tiras could be traced to the Thracians of a later period (see Gen. 10:2).

This is the brief information about the descendants of Noah; proper study of their lives revealed that all human beings on the earth today came from Noah's children. If you study their various geographical locations, you will deduce that they respectively dwelt in the present Europe, Asia, Middle East, America, and Africa. They spread through reproduction, and this is what made the world to be populated again.

Despite the flood and pronunciation of Noah as a righteous and blameless man, the satanic nature is still in the entire human race on the earth; they did things as children of Satan because that is what they really were. Thus the curse continues in the world because man lived under the curse naturally. Every one with the satanic nature is already condemned, and if you are not born again, you have that nature. The Christians have the eternal life, which qualifies us to be the children of God. We are the new creation—the people of God.

PART TWO

CHAPTER ONE

MY DEAR JESUS

B ECAUSE SIN ENTERED into the world through Adam, everyone became sinners. All mankind have spiritually sinned, and it ushered in death (see Rom. 8:12). God, in his infinite mercy, made his life available for the human race. Though men had become sinners in nature, which makes all men's activities sinful to God, he still loves them. He decided to reconcile man to himself through his only son (Jesus Christ).

No wonder the Bible says, "For God so loved the world that he gave his one and only son, that whoever believes in him shall not perish but have eternal life" (John 3:16). The Bible declares that God loved men though the world was in sin and sin was in the world. God hates sin but loves mankind; he has a passionate affection for mankind, then for him to exercise his love toward man, he gave his son for us so that if we can only believe in the son and accept the son's anointment for our sins, we will be made alive with God.

Through the son, the world that is in darkness will have light. God let us know that the world was covered with darkness and men live in great darkness. He therefore said that any man that will believe and accept the way of his son (Jesus) will have light. Any man that accepts Jesus's sacrifice will be illuminated. According to his word, nobody is counted out (i.e., everybody is lightable no matter what the condition of that entity is [see John 1:9]). All men were and are called into the kingdom of God.

WHO IS THIS JESUS?

Who is this Jesus? Who does he claim to be? What are the testimonies of God about him? Here are some of the clues of who Jesus Christ is. The following testimonies of God about Jesus are enough for every man to believe him and confess to his lordship.

JESUS IS GOD

This is a controversial issue among baby Christians and unbelievers. Many talks find it very difficult to believe that Jesus is God. Some Christians believed that Jesus is God but later disagreed and rejected what they had believed because of what unbelievers say about the subject matter. They forget that the Bible says, "The man will without the spirit does not accept the things that comes from the spirit of god, for they are foolishness to him, and he cannot understand them, because they are spiritual discerned" (1 Cor. 2:14).

I wonder why Christians can live by the theories of the world. The mature Christians do not need anybody to tell them that Jesus is God because the Bible says, "For to you a child is born, to us a son is given and the government will be on his shoulder. And he will be called wonderful counselor, mighty God, Everlasting father, prince of peace" (Isa. 7:6). A son was going to be born. He would rule; there would be no one like him. He is God. Jesus is the son that the Bible is talking about, and he is God Almighty.

JESUS IS MAN

Isaiah 7:14, "Therefore the Lord himself will give you a sign. The virgin will be with child and will give birth to a son, and will call him Emmanuel." The fulfillment of this prophecy came to reality when Mary conceived and gave birth to Jesus, the "Emmanuel," through the power of the Holy Spirit. Though he is equal with God, he became man and was planted in the womb of Mary by the Holy Spirit. We have always acknowledged that Jesus Christ is fully divine and fully human; he is both God and man in one person. No wonder the Bible says, "The word became flesh and made his dwelling among us" (John 1:14). This means that God became man and dwelled among men. It would not meet up with the requirement of incarnation for Jesus to die as a sacrificial lamb for the sins of the world if he was not a man. He had to be a man to die for the sins of men.

Thus, when Jesus lived on the face of the earth, he was 100 percent man and 100 percent God; he only did not live with the satanic nature because he was not born by the blood of man.

THE SECOND AND LAST ADAM

The first Adam was formed from the dust of the ground and with the breath of life blown into his nostrils by God. From Adam, God made a woman; both were created in God's image (see Gen. 1:26). God commanded Adam not to eat from a tree in the middle of the garden; Eve was tempted by the devil and disobeyed God. Adam was not tempted but committed high treason against God. As a result, the entire human race through them was born with a sin nature. Due to this, everybody was destined to die, and everyone stood guilty before the creator—God.

But God sent another Adam—the last Adam. His name is Jesus Christ, the anointed one of God that was born not through the blood of the first Adam. He was sent to face our penalty, to show the way by his life of obedience, and to win victory over the devil that deceived the first Adam through his life. The second—and the last—Adam, through his death and resurrection, made available God's grace and gift of righteousness. No wonder the Bible says that the first Adam became a living being while the last Adam is a life-giving spirit. He is a life giver. He came to give us something better. He gave us his life. We are born after him. He is our senior brother. He is the second and the last Adam.

THE ANOINTED CHRIST

Jesus means *savior*; he came to save us from our sins. *Christ* means "anointed one"; the Old Testament prophets, priests, and kings were anointed with oil. Jesus functions as a prophet; he speaks God's words as a priest and as a king. He rules because of the power of the immeasurable anointing upon him.

Matthew 3:16 says that as soon as Jesus was baptized, he went out the water. At that moment, heaven was opened, and all saw the Spirit of God descending like a dove and lighting on him. God anointed Jesus with the Holy Spirit. He was imbued with power. After he was anointed, he became full of the Holy Ghost; the fullness of God dwells in him without measure. He walked according to the Spirit of God. He could fulfill the purpose of his calling because he was anointed by God. The Spirit of God descended on him in a gentle manner, as gentle as a dove would descend. When Peter came to the knowledge of Jesus's identity by revelation, he said, "You are the Christ, the son of the living God" (Matt. 16:16). Jesus himself confirmed it. "The Spirit of the Lord is upon me, because he hath anointed me to preach the gospel to the poor; he hath sent me to heal the brokenhearted, to preach deliverance to the captives, and recovering of sight to the blind, to set at liberty them that are bruised, To preach the acceptable year of the Lord" (Luke 4:19-19). Jesus could do all that he did successfully because he was anointed by God. He could not do anything before he was anointed by the Holy Ghost. The same thing is applied to every Spirit-filled Christian. When the Holy Ghost dwells in you, you will become more than an ordinary human being. You are now extraordinary; you are supernatural. You can do anything with that ability in you.

THE SINLESS MAN

Jesus could stand among crowds and claim to share God's nature. He said, "Which of you can point to anything wrong in my life?" Even more amazing thing is that none of them could reply. He was the son of God. He is God. God cannot sin; sin is not consistent with his nature. Jesus does not sin. No human being had ever lived a sinless life before Jesus came. He was the first sinless man before we obtained the nature by the spiritual birth. John 8:28-29, "So Jesus said 'when you have lifted up the son of man, then you will know that I am the one I claim to be and that I do nothing on my own but speak just what the father has taught me. The one who sent me is with me; he has not left me along for I always do what pleases him." Jesus disclosed the secret of his sinless life; he made it clear that he cannot sin because he does what God asks him to do only. He always speaks God's mind, not his own; that is why everybody testified that nobody ever spoke as he spoke. The father is with him always.

In John 8:46-47, Jesus says, "Which of you convinceth me of sin? And if I say the truth, why do ye not believe me? He that is of God heareth God's words: ye therefore hear them not, because ye are not of God." Jesus could not be proved guilty by anybody because he spoke the truth from God only. He heard directly from God. Many people could not believe him just because they did not belong to God. Jesus was the only sinless being on the face of the earth during his earthly walk because he was born of God without the satanic nature.

FORGIVER OF OUR SINS

Luke 5:20-21, "When Jesus saw their faith, he said, friend your sins are forgiven. The Pharisees and the teachers of the law began thinking to themselves, 'who is this fellow who speaks blasphemy? Who can forgive sins but God alone?'" The Jewish leaders were very angry with Jesus because he declared some people's sins were forgiven. The religious leaders understood clearly that since sin is a rebellion against God, then it is only God that can forgive sin. They were very right; the only problem they had is that they did not know that Jesus is the God they were talking about. Jesus was ordained to forgive sins. He died for the remission of man's sins. We were declared not guilty by Jesus.

There would not be any forgiveness of sin without the sacrifice of death and resurrection of Jesus.

Luke 7:48-49, "Then said to her your sins are forgiven', the other guest began to say among themselves, 'who is this who even forgives sins?'" In Jesus, there is forgiveness of sin; no sin can be forgiven outside of Jesus Christ. He is the only medium to the forgiveness of sin. Remember, *Jesus* means *savior*. No one can be saved from the bondage of sin except through Jesus. God sent him to save us from the captivity of sin; no wonder the Bible says that God was in Christ, reconciling the world to himself. Jesus is the only medium by which God reconciles people to himself. He is God.

THE ONLY WAY TO GOD

Jesus is not one of the several ways because he is not a religious leader as many people think. Jesus is the one and only way to God. Jesus Christ came out not only to teach about the way but also to give the way; there is no other way to God. The one and only way to God is Jesus Christ. Nobody has ever made claims like that before he came. He is the real love and miracle of God. God expresses himself through Jesus Christ only.

Jesus said, "I am the way, the truth and the life no one come to the father but by me" (John 14:6). No one can be saved and get to heaven except by him only. A man that believes in him is said to be born of God into the kingdom of God—Zion.

This is the Word of God; either you believe it, or you call Jesus a liar. I am saying this because some folks claim to be Christians and still believe that Christianity is a religion. They believe that there are some other religions that can get people to God. They claim not to be too religious. They fail to be aware of the fact that Christianity is not a religion; it is the life (ZOE) of God in human persons who are born of God and live in Zion. Acts 4:12 says, "Salvation is found in no one else, for there is no other name under heaven given to men by which we must be saved." Jesus is the only way to God. If any man dies without Jesus, he is already condemned to hell (John 3:18).

THE LAMB OF GOD

John the Baptist announced Jesus as the Lamb of God who takes away our sins, thereby suggesting that Jesus Christ fulfilled the prophecy of Isaiah that said, "He was oppressed and afflicted, yet he did not open his mouth; he was led like a lamb to the slaughter and as a sheep before her Shearer is silent, so he did not open his mouth" (Isa. 53:7). Also, Apostle John saw a vision of Christ as the slain Lamb of God who now receives the praise of heavenly hosts, who defeats every enemy, and who takes the church to be his bride.

Paul says in 1 Corinthians 5:7 to get rid of the old yeast so that you may be a new batch without yeast as you really are for Christ, our Passover Lamb, that has been sacrificed. Therefore, no sacrifice of any kind is needed for any purpose from anyone again; Jesus Christ is the only Lamb of God. He is the Passover Lamb. He has been sacrificed for sins; therefore, our sins were atoned by the blood of the young lamb.

Never forget that the Word of God always acknowledges Jesus as our lord and savior. Recognize him as the Passover Lamb who was offered for the remission of our sins.

SHARER OF GOD'S GLORY

The glory of God is rooted in his very nature of majesty, awesomeness, and holiness. His glorious character is displayed in his active presence among his people. God reveals his glory to humanity both directly and indirectly through Jesus Christ. He displayed the very character and splendor of the Father. He is the express image of God. Jesus Christ is the glory of God in human flesh. No glory can be compared to his glory. He was God in human flesh. Jesus reveals God's glory by what he did—especially through his death and resurrection. He is now exalted in glory and will someday return to the earth in glory to go through the rapture of the church.

Jesus claimed to have preexisted the universe. The apostle John, who shared bread with Jesus, wrote that Jesus was with God in the very beginning and that all things came into being through him and that nothing came into being without him. Jesus said, "And now, father, glorify me in your presence with the glory I had with you before the world began" (John 17:5). Jesus made it clear in his word that he had the glory of God before the beginning of the world; he was with the father in the beginning, living in the glory of the most high. His death also is the greater glory because by his death and resurrection, he defeated the devil and reconciled the world to God and gave us the same glory.

THE HEAVENLY KING

In the beginning before the creation of the world, Jesus Christ was in God as the Word of God. God, Son (Jesus), and the Holy Spirit was a person; they cannot be separated, and they work as a person because that's what they are. They rule as a king. If you see the Son, you have seen the Father; if you believe the Son, then you have believed the Father. If you worship the Son, you have worshiped the Father. If you call the name of Jesus, the Father, the Son, and the Holy Spirit will answer. They are three in one God. This is a mystery to the world but a divine reality to us.

Luke 22:69, "But from now on, the son of man will be seated at the right hand of the almighty God." This is Jesus declaring his position at the seat of power. He said that the son of man will sit at the right hand of God in the place of power in heaven. When Jesus declared this in Luke 22:69, it came to reality and was recorded in the book of Ephesians 1:20, "Which he exerted in Christ when he raised him from the dead and seated him at his right hand in the heavenly realms." Apostle Paul proceeded by revealing that God made Jesus to sit at his right hand in heaven in order to put into effect when the times would have reached their fulfillment to bring all things in heaven and on the earth together under one head, even Christ.

LIFE GIVER

Jesus did not just teach about the everlasting life or tell us how to find everlasting life. He did not tell us to depend on our own efforts to have everlasting life. Jesus actually claimed to give life (ZOE). Though many Christians believe this, they still expect us to make some effort on our own before we have ZOE. But Jesus said, "For my father's will is that everyone who look to the son and believe in him shall have eternal life and I will raise him up at the last day" (John 6:40). Everlasting life can be found only in Jesus. Jesus gives eternal life to those who accept him. Eternal life is imparted into our spirits at the new birth. Jesus gives eternal life generously without the requirement of the law.

John 6:47 says, "I tell you the truth, he who believe has everlasting life." The truth about the kingdom of God is that one must believe and accept Jesus as the lord and savior because Jesus is the only person who can give eternal life. Jesus said, "And I give unto them eternal life; and they shall never perish, neither shall any man pluck them out of my hand. My Father, which gave them me, is greater than all; and no man is able to pluck them out of my Father's hand. I and my Father are one" (John 10:28-30). Also in John 11:25, "Jesus said to her 'I am the resurrection and the life. He who believes in me lives, even though he dies; and whoever lives and believes in me will never die.'"

So the life of God is in us. We are not ordinary people. We function with the very life of God. With this life, no Christian ought to be sick or be afflicted with disease; the challenge is that many Christians have not come to a full understanding of this truth. That is why the devil takes advantage of them and afflicts them with sicknesses and diseases.

MASTER'S DEATHS

It is scripturally recorded that Jesus suffered upon the cross for you and me. I imagine his death as I read of him being whipped, stricken, pierced by thorns and nails, and crucified on the cross of Calvary. His extreme thirst was because of you and me. I can understand why he would pray fervently about his deaths in the garden before his arrest. I really appreciate his dreadful suffering of bodily pains.

Brave heroes have faced death with more courage and endured extreme physical agonies for a long period of time as Jesus did. Historically, men have faced capital punishment and endured torture willingly. The fact that Jesus bore our sins makes his physical suffering more intense because sin is spiritual.

It is very difficult for human beings to comprehend any truth without having some physical concept with which to relate it for proper understanding. Jesus represents us in the Crucifixion, but it is unnatural to many folks because it is a spiritual event. The death of Jesus was more supernatural than physical. There would not have been any significance to his death if he did not die spiritually. Definitely, physical death is impossible without spiritual death. His sacrificial death was spiritual because the problem of sin is spiritual. The problem has to be solved from the spirit realm. It is the spiritual death that wipes away the sins of the world. This is the reason Jesus died spiritually. The problem of human beings is that all human creatures were separated from God. The satanic nature produces spiritual death in every human person. Therefore, Jesus had to die spiritually to correct the world's number one problem.

Therefore, there is nobody that's supposed to suffer, die, or go to hell because of sin again because Jesus already paid for the sins of the world, but people still suffer, die, and go to hell because they fail to accept Jesus as their lord and savior. Jesus bore our sentence of death. The penalty of sin is death. Jesus's sorrows, wounds, stripes, and chastisements were not only physical but particularly spiritual because physical endurance is powerless for the atonement of the sins of human beings. The atonement was spiritual.

Hebrews 9:27-28, "Just as a man is determined to die once, and after that to face judgment, so Christ was sacrificed once to take away the sins of many people; and he will appear a second time, not to bear sin again, but to bring salvation to those who are waiting for him."

From the above scriptures, God is showing us that it was destined for man to die once; here God is talking about spiritual death. Remember, it is not destined for every man to die physically; physical death is not mandatory. After all, Enoch and Elijah did not die. And many of us will not die; we will rapture. It is the spiritual death that was destined for every man because of the sin of Adam; men were born dead spiritually. Thus the physical death of Jesus Christ on the cross would have been meaningless without spiritual death. Christ Jesus went through the spiritual death as a sacrifice for us so we would escape the spiritual death. God was concerned about the spiritual death of Jesus because he knew that the entire human race was dead spiritually.

The blood of Jesus was shed for our atonement. The blood stands as his life. The blood of the master that was shed on the cross is very significant to the atonement of the human generations' sins. God warned Adam not to eat from the tree of knowledge of good and evil. They were told that they would die immediately after they ate from the fruit of the tree. The fact is that they died immediately in the spirit realm when they ate from the tree. Many folks are concerned about the physical death of Jesus, but God was concerned about the spiritual death of Jesus.

In the work of our atonement, Jesus was separated from God because of our sin. He became sin for us. God cannot relate with sin, so God abandoned him temporarily into the hand of Satan. This is why he cried out, "Eloi, Eloi, lama sabach than? [Which means "My God, my God, why have you forsaken me?"]" (Mark 15:34).

He cried out and made this statement because he died spiritually at that time. This is the reason Jesus prayed a fervent prayer in Gethsemane so that he might avoid the spiritual death. Jesus was not afraid of the cross, but we must note that Jesus was sinless and immortal; that is why he could be with God and commune with God always. Because of his nature, physical death could not have power over him; therefore, he had to die first spiritually. If Jesus did not die spiritually, physical death would not be possible and atonement would not take place. Jesus therefore had to die spiritually first before dying physically.

Spiritual death is a disconnection from God. Jesus knew the terrible consequences of a spiritual death. Jesus was facing substitution in Gethsemane. He was made sinful for us to be made righteous. He partook of sin and mortality.

After Jesus's spiritual death was when he was able to die on the cross physically for you and me. The resurrection of Jesus has far greater significance to us. It is the physical evidence that the Father brought Jesus back from hell, breaking every power of Satan. His resurrection brought us to God and ensures our relationship with him in spite of humanity's sin nature. Now in the baptism, we are painlessly and symbolically buried with him and risen with him—free from the effects of sin. Adam died spiritually; the entire human race also died from the biological birth. That is the reason Jesus had to die spiritually. He died spiritually, died physically, went to hell, waged war with the devil in hell, and defeated him for us. After these, he resurrected in victory and ascended to heaven. The whole world has direct access to that victory of Jesus. Anyone that will believe in what Jesus did and confess to his lordship will automatically validate his right as a legitimate owner of the victory.

HIS RESURRECTION

Before the death of our Lord Jesus, he knew he was going to be killed and surely resurrected. The death of Jesus amazed the people, even the disciples. In the book of John 10:17, Jesus said, "The reason my father loves me is that I lay down my life only to take it up again." This is before the death of Jesus Christ. He spoke the reality of his death for the people. He said, "I will present myself as a sacrifice to them. I will be killed because of their sins. I have a delegated power to lay my life down and the ability to take it back." He knew his body could not decay in the grave; he knew he would be resurrected from the grave by the Holy Ghost. He was persuaded that he would resurrect. In the book of John 12:33, Jesus said, "But when I am lifted up from the earth, will draw all men to myself. He said this to let them know the kind of the death he was going to die." Jesus understands the power behind his death. He knew that without his death, no man could be saved. Through the death and resurrection of Jesus, all men have the opportunity to come to God. His death and resurrection is the ultimate victory.

MASTER'S JOURNEY TO HELL

It is generally believed among Christians that Jesus came from heaven to the earth and preached and taught about the kingdom of God. He was arrested and crucified by the religious and political leaders. Three days later, he resurrected and ascended to heaven and sat at the right hand of God Almighty in the heavenly places. They believe that the death of Jesus brought about salvation and also believe that Jesus defeated Satan by the cross of Calvary.

But many refuse to believe that Jesus descended into hell before he resurrected and ascended to heaven. They argue blindly; they say it is blasphemous to say that Jesus went to hell. They say Jesus is more than a man that would go to hell. They claim to be humble and religious. It is very good to be humble, but we must be humble and scriptural. Morally speaking, it is not naturally okay to say that Jesus, the son of God—God himself, was killed by mere men, but we must believe it because the Bible says that. We must also glorify God for the death because he died for us. The truth is that his death was premeditated by God, and just as his death was premeditated, so also was his victory in hell. God was happy that Jesus died and went to hell. I am happy too. *Thank you, Jesus.*

Scripturally, Jesus descended into hell in order to accomplish the work that God sent him to do on earth. Therefore, we ought to know that Jesus Christ was crucified, died, buried, descended to hell, and resurrected three days later. "For Christ also hath once suffered for sins, the just for the unjust, that he might bring us to God, being put to death in the flesh, but quickened by the Spirit:

By which also he went and preached unto the spirits in prison"
(1 Pet. 3:18-19). Jesus is righteous, but it was the righteous that
suffered for the unrighteous according to the Bible. He that knew
no sin suffered instead for those who knew no righteousness. He
was put to death for the human race, but he was quickened and
raised again by the spirit. Before his resurrection, he went to hell
and preached to the spirits of the righteous ones in Hades. Jesus
went to hell and set free the righteous people that dwelled in
Hades—the bosom of Abraham. The word *prison* referred to
where the spirits of the dead go. The abode of the dead—that
place is governed by the devil. That is what we call hell. The
bosom of Abraham and the place of torment were in hell, the
spiritual prison.

John 5:25, "I tell you the truth, a time is coming and has
come when the dead will hear the voice of the son of God and
those who hear will live." We can see that the dead were in hell,
even the righteous, and the fulfillment of this word of Jesus came
to reality in Matthew 27:52-53, which says, "The tombs broke
open bodies of many holy people who had died were said to life.
They came out of the tombs, and after Jesus' resurrection they
went into the holy city and appeared to many people." When
Jesus died and went to hell, he set the captives free. Ephesians
4:8 says, "When he ascended on high he led captives in train
and gave gifts to man." When Jesus went to hell, he set all the
righteous people that were in the bosom of Abraham free; when
he set them free, they first of all came to Jerusalem before they
went to heaven after Jesus's ascension. Matthew 12:40 tells us
that Jesus said, "For as Jonah was three days and three nights in
the whale's belly; so shall the Son of man be three days and three
nights in the heart of the earth."

Jesus went to the heart of the earth, which is hell, when he
died. Before his death, he had prophesied about this. He compared
his three days and nights in hell with the three days and nights
of Jonah in the belly of a huge fish. He made it clear that since
Jonah came out the fish to the land of the living on the third day,
therefore, he had to resurrect from hell on the third day.

EVIDENCE OF HIS DESCENT

If you carefully study the above report, you will deduce that Jesus actually went to hell. But a question may be raised from your mind and ask, "*Did Jesus really visit hell?*"

For more clarifications, we have to examine the word *hell*. When we hear the word *hell* or when we come across the word *hell* in the Bible, we immediately think of the place of eternal damnation for those who have rejected God in this life and died without repentance. Though this is true, it is not the complete truth. The word *hell* in the English language is the same thing as *sheol* in the Hebrew language. *Hades* and *Geenna* are interchangeably used in the Greek language. Before Jesus Christ descended to hell, it was the abode of the dead for good and bad—the righteous and unrighteous. It was not totally a world or a region or a geographical location of darkness. The New Testament later gives a clear distinction of where the good people belong and where the bad people belong in hell. The two kinds of beings were separated by an impassable abyss; Abraham called it as a great gulf. The reality is that the section for the unjust was named Geenna. That is where the souls of the unjust would suffer unspeakable torment by fire and severe punishment. The same place of torment is also called Tartarus. That is the place where the wicked souls go.

Our Lord Jesus gives us an understanding of hell in the parable of Lazarus, the poor beggar who sat at the gate of the rich man. Lazarus died and was taken to the land of the dead, Hades, in the bosom of Abraham and was comfortable in the bosom of Abraham. The rich man also died and went to the same land of the dead; however, he found himself in Geenna, being tormented in flames (We must note that the rich man was tormented not because he was a rich a man. After all, Abraham was very rich, but he went to the place of torment because he rejected God before he died). The rich man saw Lazarus and cried out to Father Abraham to send Lazarus for a drop of water.

Luke 16:25-26, "But Abraham replied, sons, remember that in your lifetime you received you good things, while Lazarus received bad things but now he is comforted here and you are in agony. And besides all this, between us and you a great chasm has been fixed, so that those how want to go form here to you cannot nor can anyone cross over from there to us."

All the righteous people that died before Jesus's death and resurrection went to hell and dwelled in Hades, which is called the bosom of Abraham. The reason is because the sin of Adam and Eve had closed the gates of heaven. The Bible declares everyone in the human race to be sinners. Abraham, Noah, etc., who were declared righteous according to the Word of God, could not enjoy the righteousness. Their righteousness was just like a promissory note that gave them the opportunity to be in a special place in hell and free from the damnation of Geenna, just waiting for Jesus to defeat the devil because of their obedience to God. They were righteous, but their righteousness was like a filthy rag (Isa. 64:6). The holy souls awaited the Redeemer in the land of the dead who would redeem them by the shedding of the blood of Jesus Christ and the defeat of the devil.

God, in his infinite love, sent his only son to die and redeem the entire human race, including those in the bosom of Abraham. Acts 2:27-31 speaks about the resurrection of Jesus Christ. That Jesus was not abandoned in hell for his body could not decay in the grave. The Greek word used for *hell* in that scripture is *Hades*, which means the place of departed souls, the abode or world of the dead—a vast subterranean receptacle where the souls of the dead existed. It is the region of the blessed before the resurrection of Jesus, the inferior paradise. They were in the upper part of the receptacle while beneath was the abyss, Geenna, where the souls of the wicked were subjected to punishment. Jesus was crucified, died, buried, and went to hell to defeat the devil and take the just souls in hell and present them to God. When Jesus went to hell, he did not just go to take the saints and leave hell, but he defeated the devil and rendered him useless. In Colossians 2:15, we read, "And having disarmed the powers and authorities, he made a public spectacle of them triumphing over them by the cross." Jesus went to hell and disarmed the devil and all his demons in hell; everything in existence both in the heavens and the earth, even in hell, testifies to the victory of Jesus over Satan. Jesus did not go to the cross as the son of God; he went to the cross as a man. He went to the cross before he died and went to hell as a prisoner under the power of Satan. You must note that Satan was the head of everything that existed in hell; he ruled over people in Hades and Geenna.

VICTORY IN HELL

Thus, when Jesus went to hell, he was under the territorial jurisdiction of Satan; therefore, Satan wanted him to bow and worship him as he requested in Matthew 4:8-10. All demons on the earth and in hell gathered together in hell and were forcing Jesus to bow before Satan, but Jesus would not bow; he disarmed the powers and authorities. This is telling us about how he conquered Satan, beat him, stripped him naked, and collected his weapon, showing Satan's total defeat. Jesus triumphed over Satan and his demons and made a public show of his victory to let every creature see his victory over Satan.

The Bible declares that strange things happened that day. Jesus triumphed over the rulers of the darkness. He obtained a glorious victory for the church and over the power of darkness. He redeemed the whole world from the power of Satan. The devil and all the powers of hell were conquered and disarmed by the power of Jesus. Isaiah 40:23 says, "He brings princes to naught and reduces the rulers of this world to nothing." This prophecy was fulfilled in hell. Our Lord Jesus Christ offered the perfect sacrifice for the sins of the world by dying on the cross. This is the redemptive act that touches all human beings that has ever come to the planet earth. When Jesus was buried, he descended among the dead in hell.

Remember what Apostle Paul says in Ephesians 4:9-10, "He ascended what does this means but that he had first descended into the lowest regions of the earth? He who descended is the very one who ascended high above the heavens that he might fill all men with his gift." The gates of heaven were opened for Jesus when he ascended to heaven. The Bible gives light to this in the book of Psalm 24:7-9 that says, "Lift up your heads, o you gates; be lifted up, you ancients doors, that the king of glory may come in, who is this king of glory? The lord strong and might, the Lord might in battle. Lift up your heads, O you gates; lift them up, you ancient doors, that the king of glory may come in." Who is he, this king of glory? When Jesus ascended to heaven, he commanded the gates of heaven, which were shut because of the sin of Adam, to be opened. The angels asked, "Who are you?" He said, "I am the king of glory." He said, "I am the Lord, strong and mighty—the Lord mighty in battle." He declared himself mighty in battle because he conquered Satan in hell before his ascension. And the angels could not recognize Jesus because he had become a new person. Jesus was the first person to be born again. Revelation 1:5 says, "And from Jesus Christ, who is the faithful witness, the first born from the dead and the ruler of the kings of the earth." Jesus was the first born from spiritual death. To come out of death means to be born again.

When Jesus declared himself as the Lord Almighty and the king of glory, the angels took note of him, and the gates of heaven were opened, and the holy people entered heaven for the first time. We must also note that Jesus did not deliver those who were in Geenna, and he did not destroy hell. He only defeated Satan and collected the key of death and of the abyss. He then set the people in the bosom of Abraham free to go to heaven but left wholly the wicked and unsaved ones. If you are not born again, this is an opportunity for you to say, "Lord Jesus, I believe that you died, were buried, and were resurrected for me. Come into my life today. I accept you, my Lord. I receive eternal life into my sprit. Now I am born again." If you make this confession and mean it with your heart, it means that you are now a child of God, but if you have never made this confession before and now, it means you have the danger of going to hell if you die in spite of the sacrifice Jesus paid for you.

CHAPTER TWO

BORN AGAIN

Jesus answered and said unto him, Verily, verily, I say unto thee,
Except a man be born again, he cannot see the kingdom of God.

—John 3:3

TO BE BORN again is more than what many people think it is. To be born again is more than going to church. It is more than a state of not sinning. It goes beyond what any ordinary person can explain. It is not a religious activity; it is even more than worshiping God.

To be born again is to become a Christian. This is another controversial statement because Christianity is not a religious activity but a state of being born of God in Christ Jesus. You are not a Christian because you go to church.

Jesus demands every human to be born again before entering the kingdom of God. One day, an Israeli teacher, a man of the Pharisees and a member of the Jewish ruling council—a man called Nicodemus, came to Jesus at night to ask Jesus questions about the kingdom of God because Nicodemus knew much about the earthly work of Jesus. He knew Jesus Christ was the expected savior and really wanted to be saved. But this man could not come to Jesus during the daytime; he was afraid of what his co-Pharisees would say if they saw him with Jesus. He therefore chose to come to the Master at night and asked him how to be saved. John 3:3, "In reply Jesus declared, 'I tell you the truth, no one can see the kingdom of God unless he is born again.'"

This is because the issue of being born again is an important issue in the kingdom of God. Because when sin entered the world through Adam, all mankind on the face of the earth were automatically sinners; nobody needed to do anything bad before becoming a sinner. Sin was an identity of every human being. They were all born with the sin nature. Many things had been done by men to be sinless. Many people had observed the law. Many animal sacrifices had been made, but none of them could make men free from sin.

Sin is actually the nature of Satan that had been given to mankind when Adam fell in the Garden of Eden. He obtained the satanic nature from the devil by obeying him, and any human being that is born through the blood of man is a natural sinner. Man does not have to do anything wrong before he becomes a sinner because the satanic nature had corrupted the Adamic nature. It is the satanic nature that every human being is born with. No man can do good to be free from sin because of the nature of Satan that he functions with. We have to note that whenever a man does well, it always has a selfish trace directly or indirectly in it. The reason is because the satanic nature is a selfish nature. That is why the Bible says, "All of us have became like one who is unclean, and all our righteous act are like filthy rags; we all shrivel up like a leaf, and like the wind our sins sweep us away" (Isa. 64:6).

This is to say that no matter how good and nice you act, no matter how perfect you act, you are still a sinner because you were naturally born like that. All the people who were declared righteous in the Old Testament because of their obedience of law could not enjoy their righteousness because it was righteousness by work, which are just like filthy rags in the presence of God. That is why they could not enter heaven directly when they died; they could only enter the bosom of Abraham (i.e., Hades).

SAVED BY GRACE THROUGH FAITH

To be saved is to have the righteousness of God by faith in Christ Jesus. To have the righteousness of God by faith in Christ Jesus is to be born again. To be born again is to be newly born of God.

God wants all mankind to be saved. He therefore made available only one way to be saved, and that is to be born again. I have said it before that the identity of mankind is sin, but man can be saved from sin and come to God when he is born of God; that is what makes us to be a new person. No man can wake up one day and walk into the kingdom of God by any other means; we have to be born in the kingdom of God by God himself. To be born again is to be given birth to by God into his kingdom through the provision that was made on the cross of Calvary by our Lord Jesus Christ.

Being born again is a spiritual reproduction in the kingdom of God. It has no physical implication; all activities of salvation have to be done in the spirit realm. John 3:6 says, "Flesh gives birth to flesh, but the spirit gives birth to spirit." Man is a spirit; he has a soul that comprises a mind, heart, and will, and he lives in the body. When I said every human person was born a sinner, I was not talking about physical sin, but I was talking about the spiritual nature of man. When God says he wants to save mankind from the satanic nature, God knows that he has to give birth to us in his kingdom. When he then says flesh gives birth to flesh, he means the satanic nature gives birth to the satanic nature while spirit, which is the divine nature of God, gives birth to the divine nature of God. I know this may not be clear to many people now, but I believe we are going to get it clear as our discussion proceeds with clear and proper explanations of some scriptures that talk about being born again.

In 2 Corinthians 5:17, the Bible says, "Therefore, if anyone is in Christ, he is a new creation; the old has gone, the new has come." The above quotation means that if any man is born again, if any man comes into a union with Christ Jesus, that person has become a newly created being. If you are born again, then you are a new type of being. God has just given birth to you; that means you do not have any past. You are as new as a newborn baby in the kingdom of God. Really, you are a newborn baby in the kingdom of God. You have never existed before.

The truth is that when you are not born again, you are functioning with the satanic nature that you were born with. At that period of time, you are not in existence as far as God is concerned because you belong to the kingdom of Satan. But when you come to Jesus, you acknowledge the truth about Jesus Christ as the lord of your life; in a very brief statement of faith, you confess of Jesus Christ and confess of his lordship as a savior. You invite him into your life. You believe with your heart and confess that he died for you and God raised him from the dead; immediately God will give birth to you in the spirit realm. You may not feel anything because you do not have to feel anything to be saved. This may sound too easy, but this is the basic requirement of God to be saved (see Rom. 10:9-10).

When you are born again, the old (satanic) nature that you were born with is automatically blotted out, and you'll receive the very nature of God. John 1:12-13 says, "Yet to all who received him, to those who believed in his name, he gave the right to become children of God. Children not of natural descent nor of human decision or a husband's will, but born of God."

This is God's planned and prepared way of salvation. God planned it perfectly so that whoever received Christ by believing in his holy name and identifying with his death and resurrection is given an automatic right to become a child of God. That is why he declared that to become a child of God is not according to any natural connection; it is not a decision of any human being, and it is not according to a relationship between husband and wife. When you are born again, you are born by God without any natural or physical implication. Our spiritual birth in the kingdom of God cannot be explained by any natural man because it is a spiritual birth.

OUR PLACE IN THE KINGDOM

To be born again is to be taken from the kingdom of darkness to the kingdom of God. Any man that is not born again is a sinner living in the kingdom of darkness. "He has rescued us from the dominion of darkness and brought us into the kingdom of the son he loves, in whom we have redemption, the forgiveness of sins" (Col. 1:13).

This means that God takes us from the territory or the dominion of darkness and delivers us into the kingdom of light, the kingdom that is headed and ruled by Christ Jesus. This is what frees us from the penalty of sin and death. We are qualified to share in the inheritance of the saints in the kingdom of light. When we are born again, God strengthens us with all his power according to his glorious might. This is our victory over Satan.

Before any man is born again, he functions with the satanic nature, but immediately after he is born again, God removes that nature off him and gives him the very nature of God. That is why 2 Peter 1:4 declares, "Through these he has given us his very greats and precious promises, so that through them you may participate in the divine nature and escape the corruption in the world caused by evil desires." This means that any man that is born again has the right to participate and share in the divine nature of God. This nature of God is what makes us the legitimate children of God; it authenticates our relationship with God. We are participants in the divinity.

When a man is born again, he is newly created by God to be in a harmonious relationship with him because he possesses the very nature of God. We are now in the class of God because we are partaking of the divine nature of God.

Man's spirit is the real man. When Adam committed high treason against God in the Garden of Eden, he and every man that is born through the blood of humans became partakers of the satanic nature. "And if children, then heirs; heirs of God, and joint-heirs with Christ; if so be that we suffer with him, that we may be also glorified together" (Rom. 8:17). The real contextual information does not tell us that we are coheirs with Christ; to be coheirs means to be sharing in his glory by percentage. It may be 60 percent by 40 percent, 70 percent by 30 percent, 80 percent by 20 percent, or 90 percent by 10 percent. The real context says we are joint-heirs, which means we are not just sharers of his glory but equal participants of his glory with him. Thus, he is the owner, and we are also 100 percent owners of the glory. There is no difference between us. Whatever man can think or imagine about Jesus can be imagined about you also because you are of God, a joint-heir with Christ.

Through the blood of man, every human person is naturally a partaker of the satanic nature; that is why the Bible says, "For all have sinned and fall short of the glory of God" (Rom. 3:23). All have sinned naturally not by act but by birth. It is all mankind that have sinned by birth. We can only be justified by birth. To be a sinner is to be born of Satan. This means that every sinner is a child of the devil. The Christians are justified, sanctified, righteous, holy, and saved because they are born of God.

When you are born of God, that is what it means to be born again. If you are born again, that means you have been re-created. You are now begotten of the Father. When you are born again, you are not just a child of God but you are a joint-heir with Christ. It is not possible to separate us from Christ because we are his body; we have what he has because we are what he is. That is why 1 John 4:17 says that as he is, so are we in this world. We are like God. We are his kind on the face of the earth. If you are born again, you are a part of Jesus Christ's body. The Bible says, "And hath put all things under his feet, and gave him to be the head over all things to the church, which is his body, the fullness of him that filleth all in all" (Eph. 1:22-23). We are members of his body; we are part of him. In him, we live and have our being.

The Spirit himself testifies with our spirit that we are God's children. Now if we are children, then we are heirs of God and joint-heirs with Christ if indeed we share in his suffering in order that we may also share in his glory. The Spirit himself bears witness with our spirit that we are the children of God. And if children, then heirs, heirs of God, and joint-heirs with Christ, it is so that we suffer with him so that we may be also glorified together. If you are born again, your spirit will be in harmony with the Spirit of God, and the Spirit of God himself will harmoniously confirm that you are born again and you are a child of the most high.

Since you are born again, you are then a joint-heir with Christ; we will participate in God's glory and power. We have already entered into the possession and inheritance with Christ Jesus by faith. We are to present ourselves as real children of God that are ready to face anything for Christ's sake because we are sure of our victory in him always because according to 2 Corinthians 2:14, the anointing of God upon us always makes us triumph in Christ every day.

THE ANOINTED CREATION

I discovered in the Word of God that when you are born again, you are deep in Christ. In 1 Corinthians 12:13, "For we were all baptized by one spirit into one body—whether Jews or Greeks, slave of free and we were all given the one spirit to drink." This scripture is talking about the spiritual baptism. It is not talking about water baptism but the baptism of the Holy Ghost. It is talking about being completely united with Christ Jesus as his body.

To be baptized into the body of Christ by the Holy Spirit is to be totally sunk into Christ. *Christ* means "the anointing," thus if you are sinking totally into the anointing, then the anointing cannot be separated from you. The anointing is in you, and you are in the anointing. You are definitely the anointing. When you are baptized into the body of Christ, you cannot be removed. You are completed there.

The anointing is you. This is more than just a mere relationship with Christ Jesus. It is a situation where you are totally sunk into Christ to the level where you make Jesus the reason for your living. You are to be conscious of the truth that you do not lack the anointing. The anointing is you, and you are in the anointing now. Every Christian is supernatural, full of the anointing. Galatians 3:27 says, "For all of you who were baptized into Christ have clothed yourselves with Christ." This is a situation of being clothed with Christ. Being clothed with the anointing, nothing is left open in your body. It is a situation where you are clothed with Christ from the head to the feet. You carry the anointing everywhere you go and can win always if you are conscious of the anointing and it being in your endeavor.

Romans 6:3 says, "Or don't you know that all of us how were baptized into Christ Jesus were baptized into his death? We were therefore buried with him through baptism into death in order that, just as Christ was raised from the dead through the glory of the father, we too may live a new life." To be born again is to be identified with the death and the resurrection of our Lord Jesus.

When you are born again, that means you have been backdated to the Calvary, being nailed to the cross with Christ Jesus and from that cross to the grave and then the resurrection. That is what it means to be born again.

Thus, we are in the same class of being with God. We are partakers of this divine nature; we are actually children of the Creator of the heavens and the earth. The divine nature dwells in us; we are in the God class of being because God gave birth to us and put the Holy Ghost in us to enable us to live the divine life. The biblical truth is that the Christians are not ordinary people. The greater one lives in us.

The Holy Spirit dwells in us; we therefore are spirit beings. We must be ruled by the spirit, not by our senses. This is what will make our fellowships with God grow and realize. We must put both our soul and body into the subjection of our spirit. We are unequal with natural men and bigger than the devil.

If we can walk according to our spirits, we will be able to bear fruits with our spirits. Galatians 5:22-23, "But the fruit of the spirit is love, joy, peace, patience, kindness, goodness, faithfulness and self-control." It is the indwelling of the Holy Spirit in our hearts that bears the fruits. When you are born again, you are truly born of God; it takes consciousness in life to live the glorious life that Jesus brought us.

Jesus said that no one can see the kingdom of God unless he is born again. This has generated many questions; people always ask as Nicodemus did, "How can a man be born when he is old? Surely he cannot enter a second time into his mother's womb to be born." Whenever this kind of question is asked, we just have to refer them back to Jesus's answer: "Tell you the truth; no one can enter the kingdom of God unless he is born of water and the spirit" (John 3:5).

What does Jesus mean when he said that you must be born of water and the Spirit? Many folks have misinterpreted the scripture "to be born of water" to being born by the human parent, and some say it is talking about baptism, but all those interpretations are wrong.

"To be born of water" can be easily interpreted through Ephesians 5:25-26, which says, "Husband, love your wives, just as Christ loved the church and gave himself up for her to make her hold cleansing her by the washing with water through the word." Apostle Paul used this scripture to illustrate the love of Christ toward us and what makes us worthy to be born again.

We are cleansed through the Word of God. "To be born of water" is to be cleansed through the Word of God. *Water* in this scripture is not talking about the liquid water; it is the washings through the Word of God. When an unbeliever comes under the influence of the Word of God and receives the Word of God to his consciousness, that Word of God will cleanse him spiritually; that is what will prepare his spirit to receive Christ Jesus as his lord and savior.

When someone wants to be born again, the very Word of God the person hears prepares his inner man and will lead him to confess Jesus as his lord and savior. That very Word that leads the person is what is referred to as the cleansing water of God because the Word of God does the work of cleansing in his spirit.

THE SPIRITUAL BIRTH

Romans 10:9-10 says, "That if you confess with your mouth, 'Jesus is lord' and believe in your heart that God raised him from the dead, you will be saved. For it is with your heart with your mouth that you confess and are saved." The receiving and believing of the Word of God is the cleansing process of salvation.

The Bible declares that during this believing and cleansing process is the stage of justification because you have been washed by the water that is the Word of God. The confessing process is the period of confirmation and realization. It is the period in which you validate the price that Jesus paid for you on the cross.

To be born of the Spirit is to make the cleansing and washing of the Word of God real in the spirit by confessing the lordship of Jesus Christ. It is the validation of your salvation in Christ Jesus. It is the proclamation of our salvation in Christ Jesus that makes you a child of God. The proclamation is everything about being born again.

First Peter 1:23 says, "For you have been born again, not of perishable seed, but of imperishable, through the living and enduring word of God."

The Message version puts this in this way: "Your new life is not like your old life. Your old birth came from mortal sperm; your new birth comes from God's living Word. Just think: a life conceived by God himself!"

We are born again not of perishable seed or corrupted seed but of imperishable or incorruptible seed. What does perishable seed and imperishable seed mean?

The word *seed* in Greek is *spora* from *speiro*, which means *sowing*. The synonym of spora is *sperma*, where the English word *sperm* came from. We can therefore liken the Word of God to the sperm of man. Just as man is born from the agency of human sperm, so also the new creation is born by the agency of the Word of God. It therefore means we are born again not of perishable sowing sperm of God but of imperishable sowing sperm of God.

We are born by the imperishable sowing sperm of God. God chose to talk to us biologically in this scripture for our better and clearer understanding of our birth in Christ Jesus. When we read down that verse, we can see that the Bible actually declares that we are born of God by the imperishable sperm of God through the living Word of God.

The sperm of God here is the Word of God. God uses the word *sperm* because the Word of God, which qualifies as the seed, will have to be sowed into the heart of the man and is expected to germinate and reproduce the God kind of beings on the face of the earth. This shows that we are legitimately born of God through his Word. The Word of God is our source, and it is our life. We are born through the Word of God, and we are to live by the Word of God. The Word of God is the sperm of God that produced us. We can do anything through this Word of God.

James 1:18 declares, "Of his own will begat he us with the word of truth, that we should be a kind of firstfruits of his creatures." The New International Version puts the rendering as follows: "He chose to give us birth through the word of truth that we might be a kind of first fruit of all he created." The Message version states, "He brought us to life using the true Word, showing us off as the crown of all his creatures."

It is evidenced and biblically confirmed that we are really the children of God. God gave birth to us by his Word. This is the reason 1 John 3:2 says, "Dear friends, now we are children of God." Immediately you are born again; you are born of God. It is not going to happen gradually; it happens instantaneously. You are immediately in Christ Jesus as his body. You have to be sure and conscious of this truth, just as John was sure, and live on in the glory of the Father.

Second Corinthians 5:17 says, "Therefore, if anyone is in Christ, he is a new creation, the old has gone, the new has come." Immediately you are born again; you cease to be the fellow you used to be. Old experiences you had have gone. You are now a new being entirely. You are now a new breed. You are a new person. You are now in the God class of being. You are now a peculiar being; you have ceased to be an ordinary person. You are now a superbeing.

THE SATANIC NATURE

The greatest unfortunate event on the face of the earth (during the Adamic kingdom) was the fall of man in the Garden of Eden because it has a great effect on the earth even until today.

We must not forget that when God created man, he created him with a perfect (Adamic) nature; this is what is known as human nature. It is what qualified Adam to be able to stand and approach God without fear. The Adamic nature is a perfect nature that was imparted into man's spirit to function with. This is what ensures the possibility of communication and a harmonious relationship between man and God.

That is the nature that gave man a guarantee of dominion over any creature in the universe. As a matter of fact, the angels are to function or minister for and to men because man possessed a nature that is greater than the angelic nature (see Heb. 1:14). The human nature is an incredible nature that provoked Satan into an eternal confrontation against man. The Adamic nature is a nature of innocence. It is the nature of rulers. It is the nature that God gave to man to be able to judge Satan and the demons at the appointed time.

But on that terrible day of sin when Adam and Eve obeyed Satan by eating the fruit from the tree of knowledge of good and evil, the Adamic nature was corrupted, and the satanic nature set in. Satan stole the Adamic authority. The Adamic authority is the authority that accompanies the Adamic nature, but when the Adamic nature became corrupted, the authority came to the possession of the devil because men who owned the authority had come under the dominion of the devil.

This is what made man to become a slave of Satan. It is normal that the nature of man dictates the life of man. Since man possesses the nature of Satan, it's therefore normal for man to act like Satan. Man does not have to sin before he becomes a sinner. He is naturally a sinner because he possesses the nature of Satan. The satanic nature is a nature of fear and failure. It is characterized by violence. The satanic nature is a slavery nature. It is a nature that makes men to be mortal. It is a nature of selfishness. It is a nature of fight and hatred. It is a nature of sorrow and calamity. It is a nature of sickness and death. It is a nature of fear and crowdedness. It is definitely a nature of sin. It is the nature of the devil.

The satanic nature always looks for a way of freedom because it is under the bondage of Satan, but man naturally wants freedom that can never be achieved the way they want it. Man believes he can be freed by taking advantage of another man because the satanic nature is a nature of selfishness. The satanic nature enslaves the weaker and takes advantage of the ignorant. Man under the satanic nature reigns tyrannically. The satanic nature steals, destroys, and kills. The satanic nature is a criminal nature.

This is the nature that makes men to behave unseemly in the society and in the family. The satanic nature blasphemes and rejoices in evil. The satanic nature is a defeated nature that sought for the defeat of another man.

THE INCEPTION OF THE SATANIC NATURE

All over the world today, we can obviously see the manifestation of selfishness because of the satanic nature that Adam obtained from Satan. Starting from the friendship level, we can see that there is nothing like absolute amicability or loyalty in a relationship; we have friends killing friends and taking advantage of each other. There is no sincere relationship between husband and wife; there is no love again—only selfishness. This is why many married couples have extramarital affairs respectively. There is no absolute parental care for children.

It is selfishness that leads to child abuse and street children. Leaders take advantage of their followers. Political leaders and civil servants embezzle public funds. Terrorism is on a high level. Religious crises get more terrible every day. The intellectuals enslave the ignorant. The classes take advantage of the masses. Selfishness is the very cause of wars the world had experienced; selfishness and hatred caused by the satanic nature are the factors responsible for World Wars I and II.

When Adam and Eve possessed this terrible nature and lost the Adamic nature, they lost the direct link they had with God, so God sent them out of Eden. The fact is that God hates sin. He cannot behold sin. He is too holy to commune with sinners. God cannot commune with sinful men.

The most unfortunate event on the face of earth was the event of the fall of man in the Garden of Eden because it has great effect on the earth even until today. Romans 5:12 says, "Wherefore, as by one man sin entered into the world, and death by sin, and so death passed upon all men, for that all have sinned." By one man (Adam), sin entered into the world. Adam ushered in sin, and sin brought death into being. Death was passed upon all men. The Greek word for *passed* is *dierchomai*, which means *traverse*. Death was traversed into every human creation because every man that was biologically born came from Adam. The implication is that all men that have a biological relationship with Adam are scripturally referred to as sinners because they are truly sinners; they do not have to do anything wrong. That is why "all have sinned." The sin of Adam brought about the satanic nature, and everyone that has that nature has death in their spirit. The fact is that any man that is not born again has the nature of the devil, and anyone with that nature has death in them.

We must not forget that when God created man, he created him with the Adamic nature; this is what is known as human nature. It is the human nature that made man to be unique because it is a perfect nature that was imparted into man's spirit. This nature is what ensured the possibility of communion, the harmonious relationship between man and God. With the human nature, God gave man a guarantee of dominion over every creature on the face of the earth. The human nature is an incredible nature that provoked Satan into a rebellious confrontation against man; he dedicated himself to the destruction of that nature. The Adamic nature is an innocence nature; it is the nature that God gave to man to be able to occupy the place of authority that God gave to him.

But on that terrible day of sin, immediately man disobeyed by eating the fruit from the tree of knowledge of good and evil. The Adamic nature, the human nature, departed from man, and the satanic nature set in. The authority behind the human nature was stolen from Adam. At that point, every human being became a sinner. Man did not have to do anything wrong before he became a sinner; man became a sinner because Adam was a sinner. The Bible says, "For that all have sinned." The implication of this is because sin had been imparted into every man's spirit from the biological birth.

In John 8:44, Jesus said to some Jews, "You belong to your father, the devil." The same is applicable to any man that is not born again. Everyone that is not born again is a child of the devil. Adam came under Satan by obeying him. This is what made man to become the slave of Satan. At that point, sin nature was imparted into man. It is normal that the nature of man dictates his way of life. Since man possesses the nature of Satan, it is therefore normal for man to behave like Satan. Man does not have to sin before he becomes a sinner, "for all sinned and fall short of the glory of God."

Man is naturally a sinner because he possesses the sin nature—the satanic nature. The satanic nature is a nature of fear and failure; it is characterized by violence and is a nature of slavery. It always stands on the place of disadvantages. It makes every man that has it to be an enemy of God. The satanic nature is a selfish nature. It is a nature of sorrow and calamities. It is a nature of sickness and death. It is a nature of sin; definitely, it is the nature of the devil.

This satanic nature always looks for a way of freedom because the possessors of it are under the bondage of Satan. Because men naturally want freedom that can never be achieved the way they sought for it, the more they try, the more they improve in the act of disobedience because Satan always introduces his own way of destruction to them; thus, they do not listen and accept God's way of freedom.

Satan makes men with the satanic nature believe they can be freed by taking advantage of other men. The satanic nature empowers the strong to enslave the weak. Men with the satanic nature reign as tyrants; they steal, destroy, and kill just like the devil, their father. The satanic nature is a criminal nature; that is the reason crime is greatly increasing in the world. The gospel is the only final solution to the problem of the world; this is the reason we have been given the divine mandate to preach the gospel and bring the people to the knowledge of the Word and be saved.

The satanic nature is the nature that makes men to behave unseemly in the family and society. The satanic nature blasphemes and rejoices in evil. Satanic nature is a defeated nature that sought to destroy the human creation. In our society today, we obviously see the manifestation of the satanic nature in every area of human life because every man that is not born again has the very nature of sin, the satanic nature. This is the nature that is at work in the many political leaders that make them rule like the devil, their father.

God sent Adam and Eve out of Eden not because he really wanted to punish them. God did that to manifest the consequence of sin; we have to understand that God said he really loves them (the world of sinners). God has to save people from the satanic nature. The growth of indecent acts in the world today is just an expression of the nature of Satan in the world. They cannot do but misbehave. Men are naturally programmed to do wrong. They were born that way.

I am aware that men do not have to do anything wrong before you refer to them as sinners. If you see any man that steals, don't you ever think he became a sinner because of what he does? Really, God will not judge him for stealing because he has already been judged because of his nature unless that nature changes by being born again. He stands condemned because of his nature. Sinners do the wrong things because they are sinners and they are programmed to do so unless they are born again; even when they try to do the right thing, it will still not change them for the better.

God wants all sinners to be saved. He wants to give them eternal life. This is what brought about what is called the plan of redemption. For man to be redeemed, Jesus had to come and die for the world, which would give room for man to put on another nature that is far better than the satanic and the Adamic nature. The redemption produces the ZOE, the nature of God, and then man can be like God.

THE PLAN OF GOD

During Jesus's ministry on the earth, before his death and resurrection, he was always teaching people in parables. But he could not expressly teach the people the reality of the kingdom of God, and Jesus justified his actions. "So was fulfilled what was spoken through the prophet. 'I will open my mouth in parables, I will utter things hidden since the creation of the world'" (Matt. 13:35). Get it settled in your mind that some things were hidden from the very beginning. Those hidden truths are for the new creation because we were not in existence at that point.

Remember, Jesus was talking about the kingdom of God at that period, and the kingdom belongs to us, the church, then the hidden things are the new creation. We were originally created in God and hidden in God from the very beginning for a time like this; this is our dispensation. We existed in God at the beginning of the world, "for he chose us in him before the creation of the world to be holy and blameless in his sight. In love" (Eph. 1:4). He created us and set us apart even before the world was created. He kept us in himself for the perfect time.

We are called the new creation according to 2 Corinthians 5:17. "Therefore, if anyone is in Christ he is a new creation." That does not mean that we were newly created at/after the resurrection of our Lord Jesus. It simply means that we are a creation that newly exists on the face of the earth. We already existed in God before the creation of the world.

He made us holy and blameless before the creation of the earth; we are his special treasure. We are the real plan for the creation. "And yet his work has been finished since the creation of the world" (Heb. 4:3). We are the perfect work of God before this very earth was created. We were perfect, holy, blameless, righteous, sanctified, and justified before the world was created. Think about how great you are; you are so special. You are bigger than a mere man and surely bigger than the devil.

This is the reason it is very ridiculous to say that a Christian is a sinner because of what he does wrong. A Christian cannot be a sinner because he is righteous, holy, and perfect in his nature that cannot be corrupted.

After all, a decorated monkey is still a monkey. A monkey cannot be human no matter how much you train and decorate it. A monkey cannot be human, and no man can become an animal even though he eats and does his things like an animal. Babes crawl, but that will not make them animals. The crawling babes are not less human. We cannot by any scriptural sense become sinners. Our issued righteousness was perfectly settled before the earth was created. We were predetermined for greatness before we came. Any greatness you can imagine was made available in us from the foundation of the earth.

The great people that lived on this earth before the arrival of the new creation by revelation had a glance of the new creation. Hebrews 11:13 says, "All these people were still living by faith when they died. They did not receive the things promised; they only saw them and welcomed them from a distance. And they admitted that they were aliens and strangers on earth."

Remember, God promised Abraham a land—a better country—a heavenly Jerusalem, and by faith, the prophets of old looked forward to possess the kingdom, but God opened their inner sights and let them see the land. They found out that people were already dwelling in that land; they welcomed us from afar.

They beheld our glory, and they admitted that they were aliens and strangers in that world.

Abraham, Issac, Jacob, Moses, Joshua, Elijah, Elisha, etc., had the advantage to glance into our world—the kingdom of God—by revelation, and they trembled and admitted that we are far better than them. I don't know what you think about yourself, but I must tell you that you are far greater than what can cross your mind. You are a god. Psalm 82:1, 6: "God presides in the great assembly; he gives judgment among 'gods'" and "I said, 'you are gods; you are all sons of the Most high.'"

When last did you consider yourself as a God and rule your world like God does? God knows that you are a God, and all the prophets of old saw that same thing, but religion deceives you and makes you deny your real identity. Forget about the fact that the small letter *g* started the word *God* in the above scripture; every English student knows that the noun ought to start with the capital letter; whether a small or capital letter starts the word, it still means the same thing.

Some people even say that *god* in the scripture is referring to small gods; well, I am not disputing that. God is the big God, and we are the small Gods because he is our father and we are his children, but be sure that the scripture is not talking about idols. The same *Elohiym* that was used in Genesis 1:1 for *God* is the same word used in that Psalm 82:1, 6 to refer to us as *gods*; the Hebrew word *Elohiym* is plural for *god*, and the word *Elohiym* was chosen because we are more than one. We are many in the kingdom.

We are therefore special beings; we have direct access to God. The prophets of old tried to see God, but they could not. Moses and Joshua only saw the similitude of God, but in him, we live, we move, and we have our being.

Numbers 12:8, "With him I speak face to face, clearly and not in riddles; he sees they from of the Lord. Why then were you not afraid to speak against my servant Moses?" The Hebrew word for *from* is *temuwndh*, which means "something portioned" (i.e., *fashioned*) out as a shape (i.e., *indefinite*), phantom, or specific embodiment or figurative manifestation of favor, image, likeness, similitude, or form. Moses saw the form or similitude of God. He was favored to see God in portion, not in person.

But the new creations are special beings; we have direct access to God. The embodiment of God head are tabernacle in Christ. If you see Jesus, you definitely see God; this is not just because he ascended to heaven but because it pleases God to have his totality in Jesus.

Many of us have seen Jesus in a vision and in reality. Jesus has come into many Christian bedrooms. I had met with Jesus and touched him in a vision when he took me out of my body. We read about several encounters Kenneth E. Hagin had with Jesus. My father in the Lord, Rev. Chris Oyakhilome, PhD, told us how Jesus physically appeared in his room and gave him instructions on several occasions. If we had met with Jesus and touched him, then we have met with God and touched him in reality, not as a similitude. More so, we fellowship with God in prayers, particularly when we speak in tongues and meditate on the Word of God.

At this point, we have to make it clear that according to Genesis 1:26, which says, "Then God said. Let us make man in our image, in our likeness," the Hebrew word for *likeness* is *demuwth*, meaning "resemblance, model shape, fashion, likeness, manner, or similitude." Adam was created in the similitude of God, not as a direct image of God. Jesus is the direct image of God (Heb. 1:3). And we are complete in him; thus, we are complete in the image of God.

Second Corinthians 3:18 says, "But we all, with unveiled face, beholding as in a mirror the glory of the Lord the glory of the Lord, are being transformed into the same image from glory to glory, Just as by the spirit the Lord."

We are complete in Christ Jesus, the image of God. We (the church) are the exact image of God. As we study the Word of God, we are changed and transformed into the very image of God. We are his perfect representation according to 2 Corinthians 5:20. As God is, so are we in this world. We are his perfect representation in this world.

This very earth that we are dwelling in is not the primary earth that God planned to create for the new creation; our real earth will be made manifest after the seven years of tribulation. Revelation 21:1 reports as follows: "Then I saw a new heaven and a new earth, for the first heaven and first earth had passed away, and there was no longer any sea."

After the seven years of tribulations, this temporary heaven and earth will pass away, and a new heaven and new earth will be made manifest. That is the earth that was originally created for us. That new heaven and new earth will not just be created now or later. The new heaven and new earth have been created from the very beginning and hidden for the benefit of the church and glory of God.

They are called new heaven and new earth because their newness will not end; they are external in glory and reality. In the new heaven and the new earth, there will be no night, thus no days will be counted; nothing will grow old. Everything will be new and remain new eternally. That is the real heaven and earth for the real people. "But ye are a chose generation, a royal priesthood and holy nation, a peculiar people; that ye should show forth the praises of him who hath called you out of darkness into His marvelous light" (1 Pet. 2:9). The kingdom is Zion, the city of the new creation.

We are a special people of prophecy, predestined to own the world to come, and this does not suggest that we have no legitimate right in this present earth. If this earth is a shadow or similitude of the (real) new earth and that new earth belongs to us, then this present earth belongs to us also. We, the church, own the world. The whole world belongs to us.

Jesus has made us kings and priests to God, and we are equipped to reign on this very earth (Rev. 5:10). If the real world belongs to us, then the similitude is for us to practice reigning. We are to subdue the earth. According to the report of the Word of God in 1 Corinthians 3:21-22, it is not news that we own this present world; you might have acted as a slave and/or dependant in this present world, but you have to change your approach and act like the king you really are. "Therefore let no man glory in men. For all things are yours; Whether Paul, or Apollos, or Cephas, or the world, or life, or death, or things present, or things to come; all are yours." Get this settled in your heart: you own this world, and you can get whatever you want out of life. All authority in heaven and on the earth belong to you. Though we are not of the world, we are not slaves in the world.

The world belongs to us because we inherited the world through Papa Abraham and our being citizens of heaven. It is very amazing that many Christians are praying to make heaven; I believe it is due to the lack of knowledge of what a Christian is. If you are born again, you do not have to pray or try to make heaven because we are born citizens of heaven. The issue of heaven is a mystery to many Christians, and they are praying and hoping to make heaven. They think it is up to God. They exercise faith to make heaven; these are meaningless efforts.

Since you are born again, you are born by God into the kingdom of God just as your mother naturally gave birth to you into the world (kingdom of Satan). Just as a man that is not born again does not have to do anything wrong or pray or hope to go to hell before he goes to hell, so also does the new creation does not have to do anything right or pray or hope to go to heaven before going to heaven.

Hell is a region in the kingdom of Satan, and heaven is another region in the kingdom of God. If you are born again, you are in the kingdom of God, and then you have direct access to heaven. In fact, the present heaven is not the reason for salvation. Remember, it will still pass away, and the real new heaven will come just as the new earth will come. This is one of the reasons God does not take us to heaven immediately when we are born again. We are more productive on this earth than in heaven; it is only on this earth that you can work for God. You cannot win souls in heaven, and soul winning is the number one job of God, and we are in the business with God. We have the mandate to win the world for God. Second Corinthians 5:18 testifies, "And all things are of God, who hath reconciled us to himself by Jesus

Christ, and hath given to us the ministry of reconciliation." The onus is on us to tell the rest of the world that Jesus loves them, that he died for them, and that he wants them to accept him as their lord and savior. God wants the world to be saved, and we have the mandate to reconcile to God; this is our number one responsibility.

It is your work on the earth that will determine your place at the judgment seat of Christ—that glorious place of reward. Many Christians are escaping consciously; they want to escape to heaven because they are either afraid of the devil or lack the faith to live the triumphant life in Christ Jesus. It is wrong for us to rush to heaven; there are still lots of people that need to hear the gospel through you. You can live the triumphant life to the maximum, become a spiritual and financial giant in this world, and bring people to the kingdom of God with your money, your influence, and your faith.

Ephesians 3:14-15 says that "for this reason I kneel before the father, from whom his whole family in heaven and on earth derives its name." I want you to notice that we have a family—Zion, and that family comprises the heaven and the earth. There is no point in trying to escape to heaven or pray to make heaven; we are already citizens of heaven. You can walk into heaven when you choose to. You are no longer foreigners or aliens of heaven but fellow citizens with God's people and members of God's household (Eph. 2:9). You are not a stranger of both heaven and the earth; you have legitimate access to them all.

This is the purpose of Jesus's death and resurrection. "For he himself is our peace, who has made the two one and has destroyed the barrier, the dividing wall of hostility" (Eph. 2:14). Jesus made both Jews and Gentiles members of the family of God, and we own the whole world and the entire heavens. "So then no more boasting about men! All things are yours, whether Paul or . . . the world or life or death or the present or the future—all are yours" (1 Cor. 3:21-22). If this is the Word of God, then you can live the most glorious life you can ever imagine in the name of Jesus; you are the only limitation you can have because your level of understanding of the Word of God will determine the revelation of the triumphant life you will have and how to live that life by faith.

THE CHRISTIAN GROWTH

Christianity is a life in the Spirit, and we have to understand that we were not just redeemed by God from the hand of the devil, but we are actually born of God into the kingdom of God. But there are processes of growth in the kingdom of God as we have it in the physical realm. But our growth in the kingdom of God is not according to the number of years we have spent in the church but according to your progressive revelation of the knowledge of the Word of God that we have. You can be fifteen years in the church and still be a baby Christian.

According to 1 John 2:12-14, there are

1. children
2. young men, and
3. fathers in the kingdom

The children are the babes in Christ; they might have just become born again, or they might have been born again for several years but failed to grow in the things of God through the Word of God. They are the Christians that fear Satan and are conscious of sin. These are the carnal Christians. Though they are born again and they are righteous, because they lack basic knowledge of the Word of God, they live as slaves of Satan and sin.

Their lifestyles are not different from that of sinners, but in the real spiritual sense, they are not sinners. If you even tell them that they are not sinners, they always find it difficult to believe it. Though they are kings, they live like slaves. John wrote to them that their sins had been forgiven on the account of Jesus, which means they are not responsible or accountable for their sins. John as well wrote to them that they do not have to look for the Father through any other means—that the fact that they are born again is a guarantee that they already have the Father; they only have to grow more in his knowledge.

Young men are the spiritual adolescents; these are the people that are on their developing stage. This set of Christians are just developing from childhood to adulthood; they have started a discovery of some revelation knowledge about their inheritance in Christ Jesus. Young men are the spiritual noisemakers. They are the constant threat to the kingdom of darkness though they have not come to the full knowledge of the Word of God. But at that level, they can do anything with their faith.

John wrote to them because he acknowledges what they are doing. He said that they have overcome the evil one. At that level, they don't get sick any longer. They cast out demons; in fact, they are always in search of where they can heal the sick and raise the dead. These are passionate soul winners; they cannot do but preach the gospel and bring people to the knowledge of the Word of God. John said that they are strong and the Word of God lives in them.

The last stage is the fathers; these are the people who have come to the spiritual peak. These people do not have anything to call as a problem. They live, talk, walk, work, and do everything with God. These are the set of Christians that fellowship with God always. They are the teachers of the children and the young men. That is why John said, "I write to you, fathers because you know him who is from the beginning."

We have learned about the childhood, adolescent, and fatherhood stages of Christian life, but the fact is that you cannot just go from one stage to another without being taught and trained in the things of God. You have to practice the Word of God that you have been taught and train in it. You see, the Word of God is practicable.

As I rightly said, you cannot go from one class of Christian life to another without first passing through the teaching of elementary classes. Though the elementary-teaching classes of Christians are the basic level of Christianity to live in, you have to grow your faith in the Word of God to be a mature Christian.

The spiritual things can (many times) be understood through the physical things. In the spirit realm, there are stages, and you can only change your stage (level) through the understanding of the Word of God.

If you want to live a victorious life in Christ Jesus, then you need the Word of God, but you have to start from the elementary level of the Christian life and grow in the Word of God zealously. The dangerous thing is that you must not settle for the elementary teaching because it will do you little good. In fact, it might destroy you if you continue at that level because at that level of life, you are simply like a primary school pupil that stops going to school or a junior/senior secondary school student that stops his/her education. You know, a half education is dangerous.

This is the problem with many Christians; many have settled for only the elementary teaching of Christian life, and they find it difficult to make progress in the things of God. They are still in the same level they were in the last two, three, five, ten, or even twenty years in the Lord. You will find out for yourself if this is applicable to you or someone you know as you read further.

Hebrews 5:11 says, "We have much to say about this, but it is hard to explain because you are slow to learn. In fact, though by this time you ought to be teachers, you need someone to teach you the elementary truths of God's world all over again. You need milk, not solid food! Anyone who lives on milk, being still an infant, is not acquainted with the teaching about righteousness."

The above scripture addresses some Christians' standard of spiritual life and understanding of the Word of God; the scripture says that there are lots of hidden truths in the Word of God that have to be taught in the church, but the problem of the folks is that they are slow learners. They find it very difficult to comprehend the Word of God; they have a problem with their sense. They always want to reason the Word of God out, but the Word cannot be reasoned out.

Imagine you telling Christian folks that "you can be free of sickness" and they look at you and regard you as an unreasonable person. They might have come across that information in the Word of God, but they cannot believe it because the divine hearth looks impossible to them. They ask, "How can a man live without getting sick?" They say, "Sickness is normal," but I am glad to tell you today that sickness is not normal for the Christians.

The Word of God says many of them ought to be teaching the Word of God, but because of their sense, reasoning, and too much familiarity, the world's system has overshadowed them and they have grown in unbelief.

Though they have been taught the elementary truths of God's Word, they have no genuine zeal to grow their understanding of the Word of God and move beyond that level. They have settled for the elementary teaching, and their minds have been sealed up with those elementary teachings. That elementary knowledge causes a lot of problems among the believers; they discourage the young ones from growing. They contaminate their zealousness by claiming to know and misleading others. They even go ahead to criticize the young Christians.

The Word of God shows that people like this are immature, and they need milk to grow. Peter admonishes this category of Christians to desire the pure milk of the Word of God so they will grow. They are still infants; they are still ignorant of lots of truths in the Word of God. They require the elementary teachings again and again; they are the Christians that lack the manifestation of the Spirit.

They are the folks that are sin-and-Satan conscious instead of being conscious of Christ and their righteousness in Christ Jesus. They see and regard Christianity as a religion; they go to church with the aim of looking for God, not knowing that God dwells in them. Some of them go to church when they like and decide not to go to church when they don't feel like going to church. They cry and beg God for miracles like beggars, not knowing that they already have all they could think of in Christ Jesus. They don't even know that they own the world. They think the world belongs to Satan.

According to Hebrews 6:1-2, we were shown what the elementary teachings are. "Therefore let us leave the elementary teachings about Christ and go on to maturity, not laying again the foundation of repentance from act that lead to death, and of faith in God, instruction about baptism, the laying on of hands the resurrection of the dead, and eternal judgment."

God shows us that you are a babe if your whole knowledge of the Word of God is only based on

- *repentance,*
- *faith in God,*
- *baptisms,*
- *laying of the hand,*
- *resurrection, and*
- *final judgment.*

You are still a babe if you are still in the foundation/elementary class. He then urged those in the elementary class to leave those teachings behind them and go for maturity, which means they are immature. If you are still in this level, you have to grow in Christ. God reveals through the above-stipulated elementary teaching that the immature Christians have not come to the full knowledge of the so-called elementary teachings.

The fact is that you must grow in the knowledge of the Word of God; you must live the victorious life in Christ Jesus and put the devil where he belongs—under your feet. If you are a babe Christian, Satan will take advantage of you. You are a king, but you will live as a slave because you would not be able to take your rightful place in the kingdom of God.

THE SPIRITUAL MAN

Any man that is born again is a Christian; no one can be a Christian without being born again. To be a Christian is not all about going to church. It is not an ability to change your way of living from negative to positive; it is not even about being nice. It is all about being born of water and of the Spirit. The Greek word is *kaines*, meaning "to be born anew from above"; it is the very Greek word that is used for *born again*. This shows that the new creations are born anew from above, the very spiritual place.

The new birth is actually spiritual birth; everyone that is born again is spiritually alive with God. But not every Christian is walking according to the Spirit. Many Christians are still walking and living according to their senses and living the defeated life, which is not supposed to be; it is an unfortunate situation, as a matter of biblical truth, for the new creations to live defeated lives. The reason is that God has brought us into an inexpressible inheritance in Christ Jesus.

For the benefit of this study, I will discuss the three kinds of men that the Bible talks about extensively as follows.

THE NATURAL MAN

"The man without the spirit does not accept the things that come from the spirit of God, for they are foolishness to him, and he cannot understand them, because they are spiritually discerned" (1 Cor. 2:14). The man without the Holy Ghost has no relationship with God. He is a natural man. He is a sinner born of the devil.

He functions with the satanic nature. He is not born again. He may strive to be nice, but that cannot relate with the Holy Spirit because he is not born again. People like this cannot understand the things of the spirit; every spiritual thing is foolishness to them. "For the message of the cross is foolishness to those who are perishing" (1 Cor. 1:18). The natural men are those that are perishing. The gospel is foolishness to them.

The natural man wages war with any spiritual thing because he cannot understand it. He cannot understand spiritual information; it looks senseless to him. The natural man always tries to reason out the spiritual things but finds it difficult to do because spiritual things can never be reasoned out because they are coded in the divinity. That is the reason the unbelievers cause confusion and attack the reality and beauty of the gospel because the natural man and spiritual things are two enemies that can never function together.

The natural man can never please God in any way because he is naturally God's enemy. As far as God is concerned, such a man is a dead man that cannot help himself. He does not have faith in the things of God, and without faith, it is impossible to please God. All knowledge of the natural man is sense knowledge; his spirit is governed by his senses because his spirit cannot receive information from God.

We that are born again are the ones that can receive revelation knowledge from God because our spirits are alive and in union with God. The educations we receive in our school today are sense knowledge; that is why anyone can receive and understand it and function with it in the realm of the physical. Even many of today's theologians are sensory teachers and students of the Bible; that is why the Bible says, "For the letter kills, but the spirit gives life" (2 Cor. 3:6). This is the reason you have to be born again and know Jesus beyond the realm of the physical.

The natural man does not know God. He does not believe in God; thus, he cannot please God. He may be nice, but that does not make him please God. If he dies without being born again, he will surely go to hell.

BABES IN CHRIST

Another kind of being that the Bible talks about are the babes in Christ. They are not ordinary people like the natural people. They are actually born again, but they are infants in the kingdom of God. They are the children of God that need to grow in the family of God.

We have previously discovered that when you are born again, you are actually born of God into the kingdom of God as babes. No one was born as an adult into the kingdom of God. We were all born as babes that need to grow to adulthood stage in the kingdom of God.

We were all born as babes in God's vineyard. We were all born to be members of the household of God. But we were all born as unskillful children. It is our responsibility to develop ourselves with the pure and living Word of God. Babes in Christ cannot grow according to their biological age. The number of years you have spent in the church have nothing to do with your growth in Christ Jesus. It is a deliberate development by the Word of God. It takes deliberate and conscious study of the Word of God and service to God to grow to the adulthood stage in the body of Christ.

I have met with several Christians who were babe Christians even though they have spent years in the church. Many of them do not even know that there is anything like growth in the body of Christ. They are sense-ruled Christians.

The babe Christians are born again, but they are the children of God who walk like natural men; even though babe Christians are not natural men, they act and do things in the same manner with the natural men. Being a babe Christian is not a sin, but it is very dangerous because you will not know who you are and what you have in Christ Jesus. Babe Christians live like sinners and spiritual prisoners. The devil can easily attack them and take advantage of their unskillful Christian lifestyle and Word of God.

Babe Christians do things from the viewpoint of the world; they live according to the world's report. Whenever babe Christians are having problems, they handle and tackle the problems in a worldly way. For example, as a Christian, if you are given a report that you are HIV positive, you are not supposed to accept that evil report and see yourself as HIV positive because you are not born of blood but of the Word of God through the active work of the Spirit of God. Babe Christians believe in the junk and lies of the devil. The simple thought is that you can change any situation and always be the best you really want to be, but another challenge is that babe Christians expose themselves to corrupt and unedifying magazines, novels, and films.

In 1 Corinthians, Paul talks about spiritual things with the Corinthian church; in the process of the discussion, he was trying to come down to their level, but they could not comprehend what he was talking about. They struggled to comprehend his message, but they could not. Apostle Paul acknowledged the inability of the Corinthian church to understand spiritual information; they were born again, but they could not understand spiritual matters because they were immature. Though they were justified, righteous, holy, and sanctified, they had not yet progressed in the knowledge of God. They lived like the rest of the world. They were the sin-conscious Christians. They are the set of Christians that subject themselves to what the rest of the world is subject to. They are affected with problems of the world economy and health system, but the truth is that Christians are not supposed to be subject to the world economy or health system. Christians are special people; we were created to live according to the heavenly standard of living.

In 1 Corinthians 3:11, Apostle Paul said to the people, "Brothers, I could not address you as spiritual but as worldly were infants in Christ." He discovered that he could not address them as mature Christians. He said, "I could only address you as worldly people"; he said this because they were babies that could not understand mature information in the body of Christ. I get astonished when I hear some Christian talking that is so cheap and weak. They try to be humble; therefore, they make a mockery of the power in the name of Jesus by their way of life. They function as if the power in the gospel is not real. You cannot find faith in their words. This set of people claim to be something they do not know. They often get the wrong impression about what the matured Christians say and do. They relate to God without faith and take Christianity as a mere religion. They interpret the Bible with their sensory perception. The babe Christians are the confused Christians because their lives are not governed by the lead of the Holy Ghost.

Naturally speaking, we all know that it is impossible to sit a baby down and start discussing with him as if he is an elderly person; this is how it is in the spirit realm. Babe Christians are unskillful in the things of God like the natural men that are not born again. Just as a babe will cry before eating, babe Christians will have to cry before getting anything from God. This is not because they must cry before God can do anything for them, but they do that because they do not know how to express themselves spiritually; these are the Christians that cry while praying. They always want to impress God in their spiritual activity in order to get him to do something. Christians are born with power in Christ, but just because they are babes and do not understand spiritual things, they always ask God for power. They pray to get power, fast to get power, and act powerlessly because of fear. Any fearful Christian is a babe Christian. The Bible says, "For you did not receive a spirit that make you slave to fear" (Rom. 8:15). It is therefore the lack of knowledge that makes babe Christians fear. The new creations are not subject to fear. Fear is not consistent with our nature.

Get this clear: God is not about to do anything for any Christian because he has done everything we can require on the cross of Calvary. He is not in the business of blessing us again because he has tremendously blessed us; what we need to do is to take advantage of the blessing he has lavishly given unto us. The Bible tells us that the new creation owns the world, but babe Christians live as slaves in the world. They subject themselves to the influence of the devil. "What I am saying is that as long as the heir is a child, he is no different from slave, although he owns the whole estate" (Gal. 4:1). The above scripture is applicable to the babes in Christ. Although the new creation owns the whole world, as long as you remain a babe in Christ, you will not enjoy the glorious life in Christ Jesus. First Corinthians 3:21-22 says that all things belong to the body of Christ. But the babes have not come to live with that revelation; that is why they live a beggarly life.

If you see babe Christians, you will easily recognize them through their lifestyles. They act religiously; they are the Christians that capitalize their standard of Christian life on how to dress, what to eat, etc. They talk without faith. They believe and live according to human reports. They follow human living standards. They are Christians that confess negative things. They are sense-ruled Christians; they talk of fear and live in the depression. They believe Christians should get sick like any other persons. They can pray like anything, but their prayers are prayers of fear, not of faith. They open and read their Bible only in the church; they are the type of Christians that put the Bible under their pillow for protection purposes. When they read the Bible, they fail to understand it in the right context and will not dare to ask questions from mature Christians. They even criticize mature Christians. Many of them doubt miracles because of their immaturity. They actually love the miracles, but they are unable to perform them as a result of their lack of faith. They doubt the mature Christians that have enough faith to put the Word of God to work and produce results.

In his discussion with them in 1 Corinthians 3:2, Apostle Paul said, "I gave you milk, not solid food, for you were not ready for it. Indeed, you are still not ready." He said, "I gave you milk." We all know that babes are to feed on milk. No babe can eat solid food; you don't give a babe strong meat. It is the same thing in the body of Christ. Milk in this scripture is talking about the elementary teaching of the Word of God. The mature and immature Christians have access to the Word of God, but we do not have the same application of the Word of God. We do not receive the same level of revelation of new life in Christ. They have the onus of growing to the level where they can also perfectly live the very life of God.

First Peter 2:2 says, "Like new born babies, raves pure spiritual milk, so that by it you may grow up in your salvation." Hebrews 5:11-13 explains this well when it says, "We have much to say about this, but it is hard to explain this time you ought to be teachers, you need someone to teach you the elementary truths of God's word all over again. You need milk, not solid food! Any one who lives on milk, being still an infant, is not acquainted with the teaching, about righteousness." This scripture shows the level of the immature Christians; they are to live on milk before they grow up. Unfortunately, many babes in Christ have been receiving milk but refusing to grow; this is because they are receiving it in the wrong place. I have seen many pastors who cannot train babes in Christ to maturity because they also are babes that require milk and need to grow. I have heard some pastors saying, "It is not possible for any man to be righteous." They said we are all sinners, including the Christians. A deacon said, "We are all sinners, and we stand condemned in the presence of God"; he said we cannot claim to be holy. I wonder where they get such demonic messages; they made me ask, "What did Jesus die and resurrect for?" Unfortunately, many Christians have been deceived and believe that demonic teaching. This is ridiculous. I always tell them that we are born righteous into the kingdom of God, but they would not accept my scriptural point of view. Most of our churches are babe churches; they teach only the elementary part of the Word of God.

Hebrews 6:1-3 tells us what the teachings of elementary truths are. "Therefore let us leave the elementary teaching about Christ and go on to maturity, not laying again the foundation of repentance from acts that lead to death and of faith in God, instruction about baptisms, the laying on of hands, the resurrection of the dead, and eternal judgment." These are the elementary teachings of the Word of God. The teaching of the elementary part of the Word of God is not bad; it is very good, but we must not stop there. It must not be the church major teaching because it is for the babes in Christ only.

The truth is that you cannot enjoy the beauty of the life of God to the maximum if you will talk in tongues. I have come to understand that not every Christian believes in divine healing and a divine hearth. I wonder what you call the gospel to the sick if not divine healing and a divine hearth. In fact, laying on of hands is too high for them. Though many of them lay hands on their members, they cannot explain what it is all about. The truth is that the laying on of hands requires faith, but they are weak in faith. They know very little about faith and the anointing of the Holy Ghost. They lay empty hands on empty heads; that is why they do not have the results they should have. They therefore go on criticizing the mature Christians that always get results and enjoy their lives in Christ Jesus.

MATURE CHRISTIANS

The mature Christians are the real spiritual Christians. The lifestyles of the mature Christians are very obviously different from the lifestyles of the immature Christians. The mature Christians are the Christians who walk not according to the senses but according to faith in Christ Jesus. These are the set of Christians who know their right in Christ Jesus. The mature Christians know who they are in Christ Jesus. They know that greater is he that is in them than he that is in the world. They know he cannot get sick and can never be poor. Even when things look seemly hard, what they simply do is have a time with God by talking in tongues privately and speaking of the situation.

Mature Christians walk in love; our spiritual eyes are open. We are in a harmonious relationship with God because we are not religious men that live by worldly standards. Mature Christians know they have been blessed in the heavenly realms with every spiritual blessing in Christ Jesus. We know that Jesus, who knew no sin, was made to be sinful so that in him, we might become the righteousness of God.

Mature Christians are aware of their righteousness in Christ Jesus. We know that we are holy, sanctified, justified, and blameless. We know that God has lavished on us all wisdom and understanding. We do not lack wisdom and understanding. We know the very reason we were born into this world. We know we are a new creature. We know that we are a royal priesthood and peculiar entities. We know we are kings; we therefore reign in our world.

We know we have power and authority in Christ Jesus. Mature Christians can easily resist the devil, and the devil will flee. We know we can raise the dead and heal the sick. Mature Christians pray prayers of faith, not of fear, because we know that whatever we ask the Father in the name of Jesus, he will do it. We know how to receive from God, and that is why we always come to the throne of grace to obtain mercy. We know we have the power to tread on serpents and scorpions and over all the powers of the enemy and nothing can harm us. Mature Christians know they had died with Christ, were buried with Christ, were raised with Christ, and will be seated with Christ at the right hand of God in the heavenly realms. We put the power of God in us to walk and produce results.

We know we are functionary parts of the body of Christ; we are too important of Christ to ignore. We know we have the very nature of God in us. We know we are citizens of heaven and members of God's household. This does not mean that babe Christians do not have what the mature Christians have; the problem is that they (the babe Christians) do not know what belongs to them, but the mature Christians have gone beyond feeding on milk. We live on the solid food.

We know that milk is for the babes; we know it is dangerous to live on the elementary teaching of the Word of God because any Christian that lives on the elementary Word of God will live a substandard Christian life. Then to live on solid food is living on the matured and mystery part of the Word of God. Mature teachings of the Word of God are the critical parts of the Word of God. This is what we live on; that is why we are full of revelation of the new life in Christ. We are perpetual victors in Christ Jesus; we can never be disadvantaged.

If you spent enough time on the Word of God with quality time of fellowship with the Holy Spirit, you will be enlightened in the inner man; maturity will take place in your spirit, and you will be able to use the heavenly gift and manifest the character of the Holy Spirit by exhibiting the power of God in you.

Mature Christians are the people that have perfect knowledge of what the righteousness of God is. Mature Christians do not have any problem with sin because we know what sin is and what is not. We are never sin conscious. We know that sin does not have power over us.

We know what rightfully belongs to us and live in that consciousness. We know that we are Zionists. We know our language as an esoteric language. Mature Christians commune with the Holy Ghost day and night as we mediate on the Word of God and talk in tongues.

We know who we are; we know what we have and know what to do in every situation. We are kings and priests, and we live as kings and priests always. That is why we have permanent victory and prosperity even in the face of contrary situations. "And we know that all things work together for good to them that love God, to them who are the called according to his purpose" (Rom. 8:28). We cannot be disadvantaged. We do know. We know; we are so sure. The Greek word in the above scripture is *eido*; it means "to be aware of truth after beholding it with careful consideration." It means to have knowledge of a truth after carefully looking on it; *eido* is a knowing that is based on reliable perception. It means to see and be sure with full understanding. So when I use the words "we know," our mature Christians know I am talking about *eido*. Thus, we know that all things work together for our good. The Greek word for *all things* is *pass*. It means "all the forms of declension"—apparently, primary words such as *all, any, every, the whole, all* (manner of, means), *always, any* (one), *ever, every* (one, way), *as many as, thoroughly, whatsoever, whole,* and *whosoever.*

Therefore, nothing can work against you because nothing is beyond your control. Everything that has life and those that have no life work together for the good of Christians. Everything exists for your benefit because they were created to work together for your good. The Greek word for "work together" is *sunergeo*. It shows that every living and nonliving creature are fellow workers for our *eis* (the Greek word for *good, excellence,* and *abundance*). We therefore need to work in the reality of this truth that everything exists as fellow workers for our good. You can't be disadvantaged.

CHAPTER THREE

THE LAW

Now we know that what ever the law says, it says to those who are under the law, so that every mouth may be silenced and the whole world held accounted to God. Therefore no one will be declared righteous in his sight by observing the laws; rather through the law we became conscious of sin.

—Romans 3:19-20

AFTER THE DEPARTURE of the Israelites from Egypt through the mighty hand of God and the leadership of Moses, they went through the wilderness and were in that wilderness for forty years. Moses had mapped out strategies with God in order to make progress in their journey from the wilderness to the Promised Land after their deliverance from the dictatorship of the pharaoh.

The Israelites were God's chosen people; they were people after God's heart. But the people were not faithful in their dealing with God. They always engaged in evil things and in the worshiping of idols. They worshiped manmade gods and abandoned the Most Holy and Almighty God. They set up idols and worshiped manmade gods in the wilderness. God always persuaded them to not engage in this evil act, but unfortunately, they would go back to their evil act after some time.

God therefore gave law to Moses to present to the Israelites as a guide for their lives and means of services to God Almighty. The law was given to them to observe in order to live in God's content. The observation of the law was not to make them sinless but to make them realize their sinful living and to compel them to adjust their ways for by law is the knowledge of sin; law was the only means of defining sin. Law is a spiritual principle and a rule of conduct that tells man his wrong deeds.

God revealed his righteous law on Mount Sinai through Moses, but no one could keep God's law perfectly. No one could be declared righteous by observing the law because the law is spiritual and men are carnal. The law is righteous because it came from the righteous God. The law does not bring death in itself, but it could not produce life in the children of Israel because men were spiritually dead; thus, it was called the law of sin and death.

Jesus Christ was born under the law, circumcised according to the law, and consecrated according to the law. Galatians 4:4 says that when the time had fully come, God sent his Son, born of a woman and born under the law so that we might receive the full rights of the Son. God really loves the world; he always makes arrangements to set people free, but this must be done at the appointed time. God gave the Jews law to reveal his righteousness and prepare them for a real and appointed time for the salvation of the world. When that appointed time fully came, Jesus was born under the law; eight days after his birth, he was circumcised and named Jesus according to the law. Jesus was also purified according to the Law of Moses.

Jesus lived under the law. He obeyed the law perfectly. He was tempted under the law, yet no sin was found in him, He was sincere and the only sinless being on the face of the earth in his time. Jesus came and fulfilled the law by living and meeting up with the total requirement of the law during his earthly work. Jesus's earthly work was accurate and perfect according to the law.

But Jesus put an end to the law in his body through his death on the cross because he had met the requirement on our behalf. Romans 3:19-20 says, "Now we know that what ever the law says, it says to those who are under the law, so that every mouth may be silenced and the whole world held accounted to God. Therefore no one will be declared righteous in his sight by observing the laws; rather through the law we became conscious of sin." This scripture declares that the purpose of law was to silence the mouth of the observers of the law and no one could be justified by it. The law only has the capacity to declare men as sinners and influence them to be sin conscious.

But the new creations are justified apart from the law; we are justified by faith in Christ Jesus. The death of Jesus and his resurrection are our victory. We that are born again have the written code of the fulfilled law; that is why we are justified, sanctified, holy, and righteous. Our justification, sanctification, holiness, and righteousness are not of the law but of the already fulfilled law through our Lord Jesus Christ by faith. "For we maintain that a man is justified by faith apart observing the law" (Rom. 3:28).

This is not saying that the law that was given to Moses was not from God, but the law could not do because it was weak and was influenced by the sinful nature. God did it by sending his only Son in the likeness of a sinful man to be a sin offering for the whole world. He was not influenced by the sinful nature because he has the nature of God, so he was able to condemn sin in his body in order that the righteous requirements of the law might be fully met in us who do not live according to sinful nature but according to the Spirit (see Rom. 8:3-4).

We are supernaturally born righteous in Christ Jesus. Second Corinthians 5:21 says, "God made him who had no sin to be sin for us, so that in him we might become righteousness of God." Jesus had no sin in his life, but he put all our sins upon himself for us to be free of sin. This is the act that makes the new creations sinless. We are the righteousness of God in Christ Jesus.

JESUS AND THE LAW

In the Old Testament, another function of the law was to separate the Jews from the Gentiles. The law was not for the entire humanity. The law was meant for the children of Israel only. They were to obey the law—I mean obey the law in its totality before they could relate to God. It was the only way they could be identified with God.

It must be clearly noted that the law was never for the Christians. The attempt to observe the Law of Moses by Christians is invalid because the law was given to the children of Israel before we came and it was abolished when we came.

Though Jesus kept the Law of Moses, we have to understand that Jesus was born as a Jew during the period when the law was very much valid. The presence of Jesus during his earthly walk does not abolish the law, but his death and resurrection abolished the law.

In Ephesians 2:14-15, the Bible says, "For he himself is our peace, who has made the two one has destroyed the barriers, the dividing wall of hostility, by abolishing in his flesh the law with its commandments and regulations. His purpose was to create in himself one new out of the two, thus making peace." From the above scriptures, we can deduce many things that are very vital to our study.

In the first place, it is very obvious that the Jews were far away from God despite the presence of sin in the world. The primary purpose of the law was to make Israelites stand out and to master life and godliness, but because the law is spiritual and the children of Israel were mere men with the satanic nature, sin lived in them; therefore, they could not live and observe the law perfectly. Because all of them had sinned and cut short the glory of God, the Bible says that the law itself could not make anyone perfect. Even the Jews could not be made perfect by the Law of Moses.

Thus, Jesus abolished the law by putting an end to the existence of the law in his flesh through his death and resurrection. Jesus did this because God sent him to do it. His purpose was to create new superbeings that would live above the law and regulations. His purpose was to make the new creation a reality. God sent Jesus to abolish the law in his flesh in order to make a people of his dream, people that would live according to the righteousness by faith. The new creations are not to work in order to be righteous; we were born righteous. We came with the righteousness of the Father.

Though the new creatures have lifestyles that we call our laws, they are not the laws of Moses—laws of sin and death; our law is a law of faith. These laws function by love because we were originally born with love. It is in us from the point of the supernatural birth.

THE LAWS AND THE NEW CREATION

New creatures—the Christians have laws to live by. We are not to observe the Law of Moses—the law of sin and death.

According to the Word of God, we can biblically single out three kinds of laws that are available for the new creation. The new creations are to function with those three laws for us to perpetually live the glorious life that we have in Christ Jesus. These laws are not for any reasons different from the law of love because all those laws function under the jurisdiction of love. Remember, the Christian life is a life of love. Those three laws are the normal Christian life that determines our victory in Christ Jesus. The laws are discussed below:

THE LAW OF FAITH

> *To declare, I say at this time this righteousness; that He might be just, and the justifier of him which believers in Jesus. Where is boasting then? It is excluded. By what law? Of Works? In Nay: but by the law of faith.*

> —Romans 3:26-27

The Bible calls it the law of faith; this is the law that validated our birth in Christ Jesus. Remember, Jesus died for the whole world. He died for every human creature. But it is only those of us who acknowledge and observe the law of faith that are saved. It takes faith in the death and resurrection of Lord Jesus Christ to be saved. The law of faith is very important in the body of Christ because it is the law that validates the glorious work of Jesus Christ in our lives. It is the law that brings about the supernatural birth. This is the law that brings peace between sinners and the righteous God.

> For Christ is the end of the law for righteousness to every one that believes. But the righteousness which is of faith speaks on this wise, that if you shall confess with your mouth the Lord Jesus and shall believe in your heart that God raised Him form the dead, you shall be saved for with the heart man believes to righteousness; and with the mouth confession is made to salvation. (Rom. 10:10)

The above scripture elucidates the proper way to observe the law of faith. When a fellow hears about the death and resurrection of Jesus Christ and believes that the only way for a person to be saved is through the death and resurrection and confesses Jesus as his/her Lord with faith, it is not enough to believe. Remember, there is nothing like the law of belief, but you have to act on what you believe, which is the faith.

Faith is the acceptance and confession of the Word of God that is accompanied with corresponding action. You also have to act on your belief in faith by confessing what you believe; that is when you can enjoy your wealth and fabulous riches in Christ Jesus. Faith is acting on your believing.

Faith is constantly talking about your believing. The Greek word *pistis* is what we call *faith* in the English language. *Pistis* is the credence, confidence, moral conviction, and reliance on Christ Jesus and the professions in such things. This is telling us that the law of faith is a lifestyle of the believers that teaches you to confidently confess your belief in what God has done for you; that is when you will have and enjoy such things. The law of faith is totally casting your life on Jesus by unconditionally believing and relying on God that he is able to do what he says.

Faith is our moral conviction in the efficacy of the eternal life. Faith is all about being totally persuaded in the Word of God and constantly confessing that which we believe. If you believe in supernatural prosperity or divine health, you have to say it again and again with all conviction even when those things have not existed in the realm of the physical. Meditate on the Word of God and continuously confess it. This is how faith works. You have to be fully persuaded. Faith is complete persuasion in the divine provision.

THE LAW OF THE SPIRIT OF LIFE

The second law is the law of the spirit of life. Romans 8:12, "There is therefore now no condemnation to them which are on Christ Jesus, who walk not after the flesh, but after the spirit. For the law of the spirit of life. In Christ Jesus had made me free from the law of sin and death." The law of the spirit of life is the law that we live by. This is the law that makes the ministry of the Spirit of God real in our lives.

No Christian should live a low and defeated life because the law of the spirit of life functions in us. We have to realize that there is life in everything that concerns us. You will go a long way in enjoying the glorious life in Christ Jesus if you will dare to be conscious of the life of God in you. The law of the spirit of life talks about the consciousness of the life of God in you. This law reminds you of your life being hidden with Christ in God. I told you this law is the lifestyle of the believer. This law is observed by faith, meaning that you have an onus of confessing the life. It takes faith to live the divine life. It takes faith in the divine life in us to subdue negative external forces. This is the reason you have to keep saying that "the life of God is in me," "I can't get sick," "I can't be sick," etc.

If you have any problem in any area of your life, you can use the power that is in the law of the spirit of life and have your desired result. It is wrong for you to fail or be disappointed with this kind of law if you will dare apply this law of the spirit of life into your life through consistent confession; there is no limit to where you can go.

As a new creation, you have the life of God in you, and you can achieve anything in life. Now that you are born again, you are in the God class of being. You are not an ordinary person. You have the very life that makes God supreme in divinity. You are now a creator in this world; you can determine what happens to you and around you. Since you have the very life of God in you, you therefore can call forth life to anything you want and have what you have manifested. I challenge you to go ahead and call life into your dead business, education, family, marriages, situations, body, etc., in the name of Jesus; I am very sure that life will respond to your call because you are born again and you have the life of God in you.

Make sure that you do not doubt in your heart but have a God kind of faith; nothing shall be impossible unto you. The law of the spirit of life in Christ Jesus has set us free from the law of sin and death. Thus, you cannot be dominated by sins, sicknesses, troubles, failures, diseases, death, etc. When any of these show up, just rebuke them and declare life into your life. Tell Satan you are born again, you are the righteousness of God in Christ Jesus, and you live with the controlling power of the law of the spirit of life. You are a life giver.

THE LAW OF LIBERTY

The third law is the law of liberty. James 1:25, "But whoso looks into the perfect law of liberty, and continues therein he being not a forgetful hearer, but a doer of the work, this man shall be blessed in his deed." Any man that looks intently into the perfect law that gives freedom and continues to do this and not forget what he has seen but keeps doing it—he will be blessed in whatever he does.

This scripture tells us about the new creation that takes time to search the Word of God and takes time to listen to the Word in his daily life activities. The simple truth is that success is a normal culture of the new creation, but when a new creation fails to look intently at the provision of the Word of God, he mostly ends up in poverty, sickness, failure, disappointment, and every kind of trouble as though they are not born again. The Word of God can be compared with a normal meal we take for nourishment for our bodies; if you fail to take proper nourishment, you will end up having a problem with your health.

The Word of God is also like the manual for electronics; if we fail to set an electronic gadget according to the guide in the manual, the electronic gadget will definitely malfunction. In the same way, when a Christian fails to function according to the provision of the Word of God, he will surely malfunction. Poverty, sickness, and every other kind of negative occurrence you may see in the life of a new creation is a sign of malfunction. The Message version of the above scripture puts the rendering in a more explanatory way as follows: "But whoever catches a glimpse of the revealed counsel of God—the free life!—even out of the corner of his eye, and sticks with it, is no distracted scatterbrain but a man or woman of action. That person will find delight and affirmation in the action." This shows that the new creation has to search the scripture, stick with it and not be distracted, and make sure he applies and lives the Word. This is the description of a perpetually successful new creation.

The Bible shows that the law of liberty is the perfect law that makes man free from sin, death, sickness, poverty, disappointment, etc. The Bible admonishes us to never go away from this law because if any Christian will dare look intently and focus on the law of liberty and function according to its direction, he will never fail in any of his endeavors.

Parakupto is the Greek word for the word *look* in the above scripture, and it means "to bend beside (i.e., *lean over* [so as to peer within], *look* [into], or *stoop down*.)" This is talking about conscious effort to look into the Word of God to obtain a revelation on the goodness of God. Even the act of looking may not be convenient, but you have to look into the Word of God anyhow.

We have the responsibility of digging deep into the Word of God all the time for us to have perpetual triumph. The Word of God is his liberty, beauty, glory, excellence, divine health, and victory; the Word is the perfect principle of triumph (Greek: *teleios nomos eleutheria*). Get yourself deep into the Word of God, and be conscious of what the Word says; your triumph will be sure always.

We therefore have to be conscious of our liberty and righteousness in all that we do. Unfortunately, many babe Christians are functioning in sin consciousness; they never see any good thing about their lives. Whatever you might have done wrong or whatever has gone wrong with you, pay no attention to them and be conscious of your righteousness in Christ Jesus. The law of liberty is the law of freedom in Christ Jesus. It is the law of confidence in God. This law is the manifestation of our righteousness in Christ Jesus. The new creation is the righteousness of God, and it takes the observation of this law for us to live and enjoy the liberty of God to the maximum.

The focusing and meditation on the law of liberty is also the same thing as the righteousness consciousness; the challenge is that many babe Christians do not know the meaning of righteousness. The meaning of *righteousness* is "equity with God." The Greek word is *dikaiōma*; it is the very description of God. It is an ability to have equitable deeds always. It is the determinate feature of the act and attribute of God. The new creation has the same feature and attribute.

In that sense, no new creation ought to live below the personality of the real person God has made. We have been programmed by God to have success in all our ways; it is a pity many Christians fail to invoke this great heritage in their daily lives. The reason many Christians are not enjoying the glorious provision of God is because they live in sin, sickness, poverty, and failure consciousnesses. The new creation has the very life of God and is therefore not subject to sin. But the consciousness of sin makes many lives subject to the dictates of the devil. The power of God resides in the life of God, but it takes faith in the lifestyle of liberty to put the power to work. You have to be fully persuaded that you are not subjected to sin and its effects to live the victorious life in Jesus.

OUR LIFESTYLES

At this junction, I will like to notify you that there are many languages in the Bible that we use to communicate to the baby Christians because of their little understanding of righteousness, but strong truths are with the mature Christians.

The same thing is applicable in this book, especially this very chapter. The truth is that the Christians are not to keep any law, but we have laws to live by as discussed above. This may look difficult to comprehend by immature Christians, but the truth is that every Christian must live by them. Without acknowledgement of those laws, there is actually no Christianity. I mean, what is Christianity without faith? Faith is the very source of the life of God and his liberty.

The importance of those laws is inevitable; that is why they are called laws, but they are not to be observed like the law of sin and death. *Nomos*, the Greek word that means "laws and regulations," is the same word for *principle*, and that is what is used when the Word talks about law in reference to the Christians. In the context of the new creation, nomos talks about the principle of the new life. The above-discussed laws are the principles for the new creations to live by. That is the reason they are called the lifestyles of the believers.

At this same time, more elucidation has to be done when we talk about laws to live by because of their real nature as far as God is concerned. The three laws (the law of faith, the law of the spirit of life, and the law of liberty) discussed above were referred to as laws because God knows that that is the best way he could communicate the information to the body of Christ because of the babe Christians.

You have to understand that the revelation of the new creation is progressive; as we grow in the body of Christ, we get many things right and enjoy more of the glorious life that we have in the body of Christ. The truth is that every Christian has the job of growing and definitely functioning with principles that are discussed in this book.

Thus, we are coming to the understanding of the fact that God is not talking about *law* in the way many of us think; the Word of God does not tell us that the new creations are under any law, but we have principles of the kingdom to live by. So God was particularly talking about lifestyles in those scriptures. The word *law* was chosen in order to communicate the necessity and compulsion of the lifestyles of the believers. If the scripture refers to them as the lifestyles of faith, the spirit of life, and liberty, the information will still be accurately communicated, but immature Christians may find it difficult to live by them because they may not acknowledge the divine compulsion and benefits of the lifestyles.

A law is a rule that must be kept; a law is a regulation that enslaves the observers. A law keeps the observers under the regulation of its jurisdiction, which stimulates sin consciousness. In fact, a law is not for the righteous entities. You have to understand that Christians do not have any record of sin; therefore, it would be wrong for Christians to observe any law.

Romans 10:4 amplifies the abolishment of law when it says, "Christ is the end of the law so that there may be righteousness for everyone who believes." This is telling us that the appearance of Christ after his resurrection was an automatic end, abolishment, and total nullification of laws. The purpose of this (according to the above-quoted scriptures) is that there would be righteousness for everyone who believes and implements the lifestyles of faith, which also means that if the law had not been abolished by Christ Jesus, there would not be any righteousness (i.e., those lifestyles would not have been introduced).

Ephesians 2:14-15 says, "For he himself is our peace, who has made the two one and has destroyed the barriers, the dividing wall of hostility, by abolishing it in his flesh the law with its commandments and regulations. His purpose was to create in himself one new man out of the two thus making peace."

Jesus Christ, in his death on the cross, abolished the law-commandment regulation in order to create new men—the new creations—the *Christians*. You see, Christians are not ordinary people; we are supernatural beings. That is why we have our own special lifestyles. If you are not born again, you cannot live and function with our lifestyles.

These are the lifestyles that make us victorious always. We cannot fail in life; it is highly impossible for any Christian that lives with a consciousness of these principles to fail, get sick, or have disadvantages. We have the lifestyle of a king in Christ Jesus. We have the lifestyle that Jesus lived by when he was on the planet earth; they are the lifestyles that make God to be God.

Another truth is that no Christian has to struggle to live by the lifestyles of faith, the spirit of life, and liberty because they are among the package of salvation. They were automatically imparted into your spirit when we were born again. You don't have to pray or beg for them; they are our normal lifestyle.

If you do not see yourselves living according to those principles, don't worry. Just study this book carefully and be conscious of our nature and lifestyles as Christians, then you will see yourself live according to them by observation. You can say to yourself, "I am full of faith. The life of God is at work in me. I am the righteousness of God in Christ Jesus and believe it with passion." That is where it starts from.

You do not need any special regulation to walk and talk as a human being. Even though you did walk like a human when you were newly born as a baby, as you are grow up in Christ Jesus, you have to change your mind-set and live your life like Jesus would live. We all went through training on how to walk and talk like God just as we were taught how to speak our earthly dialect and be conscious of all that we were taught; this is how you have to be conscious of the truth that is shared in this book. As you have been taught in this book, the Bible is the final guide that you need for your life; after these, you only need to be conscious of what you have been taught, then you will see yourselves living a victorious lifestyle in Christ Jesus.

CHAPTER FOUR

DEATH

But of the tree of the knowledge of good and evil, thou shalt not eat of it: for in the day that thou eatest thereof thou shalt surely die.

—Genesis 2:17

D*EATH*, ACCORDING TO the *Oxford Advanced Learner's Dictionary*, can be defined as "the fact of somebody dying or being killed." It can be referred to as the end of life. Some folks regard death as one of the fallen angels that fell with Lucifer. They say death was created by God but not for killing people in the first place but for service to God. They say he changed his status and corrupted his anointing just like Lucifer did.

But nobody has scripture for that. Death is not a creature contrary to what many folks believe. Death is not one of the fallen angels because it was not among the original plan of God. Many folks even think death is an agent of God because of some figurative expression that God used in the Bible regarding some of death's activities. They fail to recognize that death is an enemy of God. "The last enemy to be destroyed is death" (1 Cor. 15:26).

Death is spiritual. "For when you eat of it you will surely die" (Gen. 2:17). This does mean that God anticipated death; God made that statement to notify Adam the consequence of falling. God knew that the law of death existed in Satan, and anyone that falls will inherit that law from him automatically as a nature. For example, life is a law that exists in the Spirit of God, and anyone that has the nature of God has life in his nature. Therefore, death is a nature just as life is a nature of God, and death is a nature of Satan.

It must be noted that the nature of death is the same thing as the satanic nature or sin nature, and this nature does not kill; it only makes death possible. It gives people the ability—an enablement to die at their own will, which means that men can decide not to die even with the very nature of death that is present in their spirits. Satan only takes advantage of people's choices to kill them even when they do not really want to die.

Originally, death worked in agreement with any man that would die. No man can die without him/her agreeing with death. The truth is that man must return to the dust as a consequence of Adam's sin, but man still has a legitimate power to know and decide when to return to the dust.

The Hebrew word for *death* is *muwth*, meaning "to die." It indicates a natural death in peace at an old age, as in the in case of Abraham. Abraham was a good example in Genesis 25:8. Violence later characterized death because of the ignorance of man; it means that men do not really have to struggle before dying.

Before the resurrection of our Lord Jesus Christ, every man had the very nature of death, but there were some people that knew the limitation of the power of death and took advantage of its limitation and refused to die. Elijah had the nature of death just like anybody else, but he refused to die. If death could kill anyone, it could have killed Elijah in order to hinder the plan of God.

If close attention is given to the study of the life of Elijah, you will discover that he had many threats of death in life; he at a point in time wanted to agree to die, but God spoke to him to encourage him, and he later decided not to die. This is not because he was a prophet; after all, many prophets died before him, during his time, and after him. Elijah knew when he ought to be with the Lord and went to catch his flight when the time came. "Suddenly a chariot of fire and horses of fire appeared and separated the two of them, and Elijah went up to heaven in a whirlwind" (2 Kings 2:11).

In the book of the beginning, it is said, "Enoch walked with God; then he was no more, because God took him away" (Gen. 5:24). Enoch walked with God in faith, and God took him when it was time for him to be with the Lord. "By faith Enoch was taken from this life, so that he did not experience death; he could not be found, because God had taken him away. For before he was commended as one who pleased God. And without faith it is impossible to please God" (Heb. 11:5-6). The above scripture tells us that the secret behind the immortality of Enoch is his faith. Enoch had faith that he would live and not experience death, and it happened just the way he wanted it. For more clarification, the Greek word for *faith* is *pistis*, which means the persuasion, credence, moral correction, or reliance upon Christ for salvation and the constancy in such profession.

Enoch did not live in the time of Christ; thus, his faith was not reliant upon Christ for salvation because Jesus had not come when he lived, but he relied upon God, father of our Lord Jesus Christ, for immortality. He had moral conviction on his immortality and was very constant or consistent in such a confession. In other words, he continued confessing that he would not die and live to be taken up by God. Death must have intimidated Enoch through sickness or any other of its threats as he did to Elijah and every other human person, but Enoch refused to be intimidated.

Enoch was a man of faith. He lived in faith and was conscious of what God could do. He was diligent enough that he taught Methuselah, his son, to live a life of faith. Methuselah lived in faith and lived the longest in years on the planet earth.

Deuteronomy 30:19 says, "This day I call heaven and earth as witness against you that I have set before you life and death, blessings and curses." The whole universe witnesses that life and death are optional. This is what Enoch and Elijah took advantage of; they chose life and refused to die.

When God created Adam, he gave dominion to Adam, and the same thing is applicable to every human being on the planet earth, but when Adam committed high treason against God, he lost his dominion and was subjected to Satan. And because man was subjected to Satan, man inherited death from him, but God, on the grant of justice, notifies us that we have the right to choose not to die even though we inherited death in our spirits. That is why God said, "Therefore chose life" (Deut. 30:19).

There were many other great men that lived in the Old Testament, but they died like kings would die. None of them died sudden or violent deaths. So if you must die, then die like Abraham who knew when he would die and blessed his son before he died. When he wanted to die, he gave all that he owned to Isaac and breathed his last breath. He died at a very good old age; he died when he was fully satisfied (Gen. 25:8).

I can recommend Isaac's death for anyone that is fully satisfied with living. In Genesis 35:29, Jacob died a beautiful death. He gave instructions of where he must be buried. Having given all the necessary instructions to his sons, he properly arranged his body on the bed, breathed his last, and departed the mortal body. "And he charged them, and said unto them, I am to be gathered unto my people: bury me with my fathers in the cave that is in the field of Ephron the Hittite, And when Jacob had made an end of commanding his sons, he gathered up his feet into the bed, and yielded up the ghost, and was gathered unto his people" (Gen. 49:29, 33).

Before Aaron would die, God had to conduct a meeting with him and Moses. Aaron could not die just in any way. God called Moses and Aaron for a meeting at Mount Hor near the border of Edom. The Lord said to Moses and Aaron that Aaron would be gathered to his people. God did not kill Aaron. He notified him that it was time for him to relocate to the bosom of Abraham (Hades). At that period, Aaron was not even afraid. The departure process was done on Mount Hor. They went up Mount Hor. Moses removed Aaron's garments and put them on his son Eleazar. And Aaron died there on top of the mountain (Num. 20:22-29).

Moses also died this kind of beautiful death in Deuteronomy 34:1-7. God called Moses for a meeting, the same thing he did to Aaron. The venue was Mount Nebo from the plains of Moab to the top of Pisgah. The first item on the agenda was the reality of the Promised Land that was promised in the oath to Abraham, Isaac, and Jacob.

The second item on the agenda was that Moses would not enter the Promised Land. He could only see the land just as he died, then he died after the meeting, and God buried him. These were men that had death in their spirits, but they died beautiful deaths, not violent. They were able to subdue the power of death by faith. Daniel could not be killed by violent lions because he was conscious of the presence of angels by faith. He refused to recognize the presence of the lions that he saw with his optical eyes.

Shadrach, Meshach, and Abednego faced death but could not be killed by the scorching furnace because they were fully conscious of the presence of God—even in the fire. Their secret is faith. If all these happened in the Old Testament, the greater ones can happen in the new life.

THE ORIGIN OF DEATH

And the Lord God commanded the man, saying, of every tree of the garden thou mayest freely eat. But of the tree of the knowledge of good and evil, thou shalt not eat of it: for in the day that thou eatest thereof thou shalt surely die.

—Genesis 2:16-17

God created man and put him in the Garden of Eden for pleasure and to reign and have dominion over all the creatures on the face of the Earth. But he showed him a particular tree in the middle of the garden and commanded him not to eat of it because the day he ate of it was the day he would die.

This shows that the day Adam ate the fruit was the day death began on earth. Immediately after Adam and Eve ate from the tree of the knowledge of good and evil, they died. One thing that always confuses many folks is that Adam and Eve did not fall and die physically, but as far as God was concerned, they died immediately, including all other human beings that would be born through them. When God created Adam and Eve, he created in them a biological law for the purpose of reproduction, and that biological law also died instantaneously, so whoever comes through them died from birth; thus, any man that comes from the biological law is born dead.

The point is that there are three kinds of deaths that work hand in hand. They are the following:

o *Physical death*
o *Spiritual death*
o *Everlasting death*

The physical death is the kind of death that many people know, but that is not the first death. Physical death is the second death. Physical death is what many people expect to had taken place when Adam and Eve ate the fruit. The physical death is a departure of the human spirit from his/her body. When God said "For dust you are and to dust you will return" (Gen. 3:19), he was talking about the physical death, but it was impossible without the spiritual death because the spiritual death is what enables the physical death. Remember, the physical is included in the spiritual.

The spiritual death is the first death. The spiritual death is the separation of man from God; it is the termination of the relationship between man and God. It is not talking about God rejecting man totally. It is not a creation of enmity between man and God because the Bible tells us that God loves the human creature, but he was separated from God because he possesses the nature of Satan. Spiritual death is not the will of God but is the fruit of disobedience. This is the death that made Adam and Eve die immediately when they ate the fruit, and every human being was born into this state except Jesus. This is what makes the physical death possible. The spiritual death is a nature in man that enables him to die. Spiritual death is what is known as mortality.

The eternal death is called the final death. It is the eternal condemnation of those that fail to accept the lordship of our Lord Jesus Christ before they die. Those that died before the resurrection of Jesus Christ and did not go to the bosom of Abraham will die the eternal death because they did not keep the law and failed to believe in the revelation of the coming Jesus.

The eternal death is the eternal separation from God without any possibility of remedy. The lake of fire is the final/eternal death (Rev. 20:14). Every man that died without Christ goes to hell, and at the final judgment, the whole of hell and everything that possesses death will be thrown into the lake of fire.

THE REIGN OF DEATH

Nevertheless death reigned from Adam to Moses, even over them that had not sinned after the similitude of Adam's transgression, who is the figure of him that was to come.

—Romans 5:14

Death came into existence as a result of the sin of Adam. But at that time, no record of an act of sin was made. They all had the sin nature that made them to be sinners by nature; they were sinners naturally, but sin was not taken into account. It was not that their sins were forgiven. God only decided not to make an account of it, but death used that medium to reign over the people. However, God is not just only having problems with the act of sin. He actually has a problem with the nature of sin. There is therefore no point for an account of sin by God. Sinners are sinners anyhow.

From the time Adam ate from the tree of good and evil, death reigned like a king over human beings. The Greek word used for *reign* in this scripture is *basileuo*, meaning "to rule." Death definitely ruled the world at that period. It was the king of the world, in the sense of it, figuratively. It legally exercised dominion over people. This is where violence came in; it forced them to accept its dominion. Nobody wanted to die, but they could not decide not to die even though they had a legal right to choose to live or die. The truth remains that physical death was not mandatory. It is the spiritual death that is mandatory for every human being. The only person that refused to be forced to die is Enoch during the time that death reigned.

From the time of Adam to the time of Moses, death had the legitimate power to kill any man according to the agreement of that man, but because death is satanic, it functions in illegitimacy; it forces people to agree with its operation though it does that diplomatically. Every man ought to die like how Abraham and Isaac died. But death uses the ignorance of men about this truth and deceives them into believing that death is a debt that man must pay at any time it requires it. Death makes every human creature to believe that all human beings are in its hand; the truth is that he does not have the power to end any man's life.

He also injected the spirit of fear into every human being. Death functions with fear; it makes man to be conscious of its activities in fear. Hebrews 2:15 talks about those who, all their lives, were held in slavery by their fear of death. The Greek word for *fear* in the scriptures is *phobos* from *phobomai*, meaning "to be put in fear or fright." In other words, death frightens. It makes people to be unnecessarily terrified. The law of nature teaches that fear is faith in the existence and power of what you fear; this is what made death reign like a king from the time of Adam to Moses.

God was not happy with the scenario, then God introduced law, and whosoever keeps the law will live. But the inability of man to keep the law made death to continue its satanic activities and perpetually subject all to the devil. Law is spiritual, but human beings were carnal; thus, they could not take the advantage of all the spiritual goodness in the law. Instead of keeping the law, they break the law. From that time, the law started working against them. God started taking an account of their sins, and Satan continuously accuses them for their wrong. Death adopted sin as its sting and law as the power of sin. The law empowered sin, and sin was adopted by death as its sting. Sin was the major poison that death used to kill people. God did not give law to enhance the activities of death, but because men were unable to take advantage of the law, death was smart enough to take advantage of man's ignorance and used the law against the human creatures.

But in the mind of God and also in the legal ground, death stopped reigning when the law was given; it was the ignorance of that truth that makes death parade itself as a king. God stopped it from reigning when he gave the law to Moses. Moses and Aaron were aware of this spiritual truth, which is why God had to conduct a meeting with them before they died respectively. The introduction of law did not eradicate death; it did not mean that man must not die because it did not give immortality, but it came with the principle of dying at an old age according to your decision.

MASTERS OVER DEATH

One of the mysteries that the church has not come to capitalize on is that when God defeated the devil and delivered the world to us, death was one of those things that dwelled in the world and was subjected to us as our slave. The biblical truth is that death is just like a servant in our care that we can determine its activity. Death has no legitimate right to kill any Christian because death is subject to us. When you as a Christian discover that you have finished your purpose on the earth and decide to be with the Lord, then you can call on death to ride on it like a horse to heaven in any way you want; it's just like how Abraham and Isaac did. You can decide to ride death like a horse to heaven like R. W. Shambach, who laughed with the Holy Ghost when he was going to heaven. You may also decide to be killed for the sake of the gospel like the early apostles.

Apostle Paul could not be killed until he accomplished his purpose on earth. There was a period that Paul felt like going to heaven; he was contemplating on whether to go or not. He later decided to stay for the benefit of the church. He made it clear that going to heaven was the best choice, but for the benefit of the church that would miss his preaching, he stayed behind. When he was through with them, he said, "For I am already being poured out like a drink offering, and the time has come for my departure." "For I am now ready to be offered, and the time of my departure is at hand" (2 Tim. 4:6, KJV). The Message version stipulates as follows: "You take over. I'm about to die, my life an offering on God's altar" (2 Tim. 4:6, MSG).

What impressive words. He had already been poured out like a drink offering. This means that he had fulfilled his purpose on the face of the earth to its totality. He utilized all his potential for the benefit of humanity and the kingdom of God. He said, "I have fought the good fight, I have finished the race, I have kept the faith" (2 Tim. 4:7). This is the real Christian life. You may be asking in your mind, "Why were the apostles killed brutally if death is subject to the Christians?" The answer to that question is that they decided to die as martyrs. They found joy in being killed for the sake of the gospel. I love it too.

They know that it is more rewarding in heaven to die for the sake of the gospel. Paul was persuaded not to go to Jerusalem because he would be seized and jailed, but he responded that he was not going to be jailed only. He said that he was also ready to be put to death. His mission was to go there and die as a martyr.

If you do not want to die like that, you can die like R. W. Shambach or be taken away like Elijah and Enoch, or you can decide to live till Jesus comes for the rapture of the church. But be conscious of the fact that you own death as your subject. "So then, no more boasting about men! All things are yours, whether Paul or Apollos or cephas or the worlds or life or <u>death</u> or the present of the future—all are yours" (1 Cor. 3:21-22). If all things are really yours, then you can use all things for your benefit respectively. However, there is nowhere in the Bible that says you must die before going to heaven. Do not worry if it has happened to someone or not. The fact is that you can go just as Enoch and Elijah left if you choose to. The fact that nobody has dared to grow his/her faith to this level does not mean it is not possible. I will show you how possible it is from the Bible in this book.

DEATH IS CONQUERED

Death is a defeated enemy. When Jesus defeated the devil, he conquered death also. "For we know that since Christ was raised from the dead, he cannot die again; death no longer has mastery over him" (Rom. 6:9). Get to know that when you see the word *Christ*, God is not talking about Jesus only. He is talking about Jesus and the church (you and me) as one body because by one spirit were we baptized into one body, the body of Christ (1 Cor. 12:13). "And God placed all things under his feet and appointed him to be head over everything for the church, which is his body, the fullness of him who fills everything in every way" (Eph. 1:2-23).

God placed all things, including death, under Christ's feet, and he appointed Jesus as the head and the church as the body; we (Jesus and the church) are together far above everything. This one body is anointed by God and called Christ. Thus, be observant; when you see the word *Christ* in the Bible, God is actually talking about you and Jesus as an anointed body. If you are born again, then you are a body of Christ.

Now if we died with Christ, we believe that we will also live with him. If we died in this one body, we therefore believe that we will also live with Jesus, our supreme head, for we know that since Christ was raised from the dead, he cannot die again; death no longer has mastery over us. In the mind of God, we died, went to hell, and defeated the devil; we resurrected, ascended to heaven, and are now seated at the right hand of God with Jesus.

The death and resurrection of Jesus is the victory over death because sin was nailed on the cross when he was crucified. "The sting of death is sin" (1 Cor. 15:56) and "You have been set free from sin and have become slaves of righteousness" (Rom. 6:18). We have been made free, librated, and exempted from sin. We are free from the sting of death; it cannot harm us on a legal ground. Sin is a nature, and we have been exempted from that nature; righteousness was injected into our spirit. In view of that, the sting of death/sin is useless in our world—Zion. "He himself bore our sins in his body on the tree, so that we might die to sins and life for righteousness; by his wounds you have been healed" (1 Pet. 2:24).

If you are dead to sin, you can't live for or in it again; you have passed that level. You now live for and in righteousness, then sin does not have power over you again (Rom. 6:14). You live in righteousness, and it produces life in you; it is the nature of God in you.

Sin itself has no power again because law was the power of sin. "And the power of sin is the law" (1 Cor. 15:56). And law has no effect in this dispensation of grace. "For he is our peace, who hath made both one, and hath broken down the middle wall of partition between us; having abolished in his flesh the enmity, even the law of commandments contained in ordinances; for to make in himself of twain one new man, so making peace;" (Eph. 2:14-15). Jesus abolished the law and its commandments and regulations in his body. The purpose was to create the new creations that are superior to the devil, having death under their feet.

Jesus exempted us from sin, rendered sin useless, and abolished the law in order to make it impossible for sin to have power over us again. Thus, death was rendered useless, powerless, and defeated in this generation.

Jesus said, "I am the living one; I was dead and behold I am alive forever and ever! And I hold the keys of death and Hades" (Rev. 1:18). "But it was now been revealed through the appearing of our savior, Christ Jesus, who has destroyed death and has brought life and immortality to light through the gospel" (2 Tim. 1:10). The Greek word used for the word *destroyed* in this passage is *katargeo*, which means "to be rendered entirely idle or useless."

Death had been rendered entirely idle (useless). It had been abolished, ceased, destroyed, done away with, became of no effect, and became naught. Death has failed; it has been made void. Death is inactive and ineffective in the real sense of it. If you hear or see any man dead, just know that that man gave the power to death at that moment to kill him. The power of death is the fear of death; fear empowers death. Having known this, you can decide not to die until you are fully satisfied with your life. You decide to go to heaven at your own will or live till the rapture of the church takes place.

DIVINE HEALTH

Having been convinced about the immortal life, you may be confused about how to live the life of God to the fullest because of fear of old age. You may be wondering of how to cope when you are really old. But the Bible shows that old age is not applicable to the new creation because Zion is a timeless zone.

You can number your years because you are on the earth, but that should not determine your health. "But he was wounded for our transgressions, he was bruised for our iniquities: the chastisement of our peace was upon him, and with his stripes we are healed" (Isa. 53:5). Long before the birth of Jesus Christ, Isaiah prophesized the birth, life, death, and resurrection of Jesus and the glory thereafter. If you study the Isaiah 53:5 quoted above, you will concur with me that Jesus had settled everything that pertains to your health from the day you were born again till the day you will decide to depart, and if you would like to wait behind till the rapture, there have been made provisions for that. In other words, Jesus carefully arranged for your good, healthy, strong, and beautiful old age from the above scriptures. God does not expect you to be sick and start looking or praying for healing.

He does not want you to get sick at all. If you notice, God did not say, "With his stripes we are heal." Rather, he said, "With his strips we are healed." The word *healed* is in the past tense, meaning that you are sickness-free. You are far away from sickness. Sickness is not consistent with your nature. If you ever get sick, just backdate yourself into the above scripture and remain healed; that is the life Jesus Christ brought for us: a divine health—living without sickness. Third John 1:2 shows God's mind about your health, then you can choose to live the divine life that Jesus brought for us 24 hours a day, 7 days a week, 365 days a year, and every moment you spend on earth.

In Romans 11, the Bible says, "But if the spirit of him that raised up Jesus from the dead dwell in you, he that raised up Christ from the dead shall also quicken your mortal bodied by his spirit that dwelt in you." If you are born again and filled with the Holy Ghost, then the same spirit that raised Jesus from the dead dwells in you, and that spirit daily quickens your body. You do not require external influence; you already have the internal quickener inside of you. The Greek word for *quicken* is *zoopoic*, which means "to revitalize (literally or figuratively); to make alive, give life, or quicken; to give life to the dead; or to recall to life." In other words, your body does not have a problem of weakening; the Holy Ghost revitalizes it every day. The Holy Spirit will vitalize your body even when you are 120 and above.

The secret of divine health is in the Word of God. Proverbs 4:20-22 says, "My son, attend to my words; incline thine ear unto my sayings. Let them not depart from thine eyes; keep them in the midst of thine heart. For they are life unto those that find them, and health to all their flesh." The Hebrew word for *health* here is *marpe*, meaning *curative* (i.e., a medicine). This means the Word of God is a medicine for your body.

You can live a sickness-free life by getting yourself submerged into the Word of God and being conscious of the vitalization of the Holy Ghost. Remember, "No one living in Zion will say, 'I am ill'" (Isa. 33:24). We don't get sick in Zion; what the devil does is to make you think you are sick when you feel some symptoms and make you accept the ailment by having you confess the sickness, and then you will be afflicted. As a new creation, you can't be sick even when you feel any symptoms; all you have to do is to talk to the symptoms, call them by their names, and ask them to go away from your body in the name of Jesus, then ignore the symptoms. Don't be among them that celebrate sickness; whatever is not consistent with the gospel should be immediately rejected, and you must change the situation to what you wish to see in your life. You must not allow anything you don't want to see in your life; resist it and cast it out of your body. You can do the same thing with poverty because they are all agents of the devil.

THE ETERNAL LIFE

We learned that the people in the Old Testament could live their lives to the maximum and die whenever they decided to die. Even those that are not born again today can still live to the maximum and die whenever they want to die. Though God does not want them to die without them being born again because no matter how long they live, they will still go to hell if they die without being born again.

But in the new life, the case is better compared to that of the Old Testament. In the new life in Christ Jesus, death has been conquered and abolished. It must be noted that death was part of the old life; any man that was not born again had the nature of death, and thus, they had to die. Enoch and Elijah, who escaped death by faith, will still come back to this earth and die after their assignment during the last three and one-half years of tribulation.

But they will resurrect and ascend to heaven just as Jesus did. But that is not applicable to the new man in Christ. A man in Christ can live and decide not to die till the rapture takes place. Remember, millions of Christians all over the world will be alive during the rapture of the church; we will rapture with him, never experiencing death because we have the eternal life.

The Bible says, "Just as Moses lifted up the snake in the desert, so the son of Man must be lifted up, that everyone who believes in him may have eternal life" (John 3:15). The son of man, Jesus Christ, must be lifted up so that everyone who believes in him may have eternal life. Obviously, Jesus was lifted on the cross, died, went to hell, defeated the devil, resurrected, ascended, and sat at the right hand of God. Anyone that believes in him and accepts his lordship has the eternal life. The Greek word *eternal* is *aionios*, meaning "perpetual or continuing for a long period of time without interruption." And the Greek word for *life* is *zoë*, meaning *life*—not just a life but a life of bliss and glory in the kingdom of God. It is a blessed and satisfying life without an end. It is the God kind of life. It is the life that contains all the glorious goodies that God enjoys. This is the life Jesus brought for us, and we have that life now. "Whosoever believe in him shall not perish but have eternal life" (John 3:16). The Greek word for *perish* here is *apollum*, which means "to be destroyed fully" or "to perish, lose, mar, or die." In other words, if you are born again, you are not programmed to be destroyed, perish, be lost, be marred, or die because you do have the perpetual, blissful, blessed, and satisfying life that has no end.

Thus, every Christian has the legitimate right to live the blissful, glorious, blessed, and satisfied life till the rapture takes place. You can live as long as you choose to without being worn out because divine health is part of the eternal life. Third John 1:3 says, "Dear friend, I pray that you enjoy good the . . ." Good health is our inheritance; it is part of eternal life. "No one living in Zion will say, 'I am ill'" (Isa. 33:24). Zion is the kingdom of God, and anyone that is born again is born of God in Zion; therefore, you are not supposed to be sick as a Christian. The truth is that you can be as strong as fifty at the age of 120 years and live the blissful, glorious, blessed, and satisfying life that Jesus brought for us. In the realm of the spirit, old age does not exist. God has been living before the very beginning and has never grown old because he lives with ZOE in Zion, and Zion is a timeless zone.

The problem of many Christians is Hebrews 9:27 that says, "Just as man is destined to die once, after that to face judgment." They erroneously capitalize on this verse and interpret it wrongly. They say every man is destined to die and face judgment. The error is the interpretation; they fail to study the passage closely. God is actually talking about every human creation born by human beings that have been dead spiritually at the point of their birth and automatically sentenced to struggle as sinners under the influence of the devil.

Christians are not included because Jesus was judged and sentenced to death for us and we were passed from death to life. We were not born by the blood of man; we were born of God himself. "Therefore, there is now no condemnation for those who are in Christ Jesus" (Rom. 8:1). The Greek word for *condemnation* in that Romans 8:1 is *katakrima*, which means "adverse sentence." It was derived from *katakrino*, meaning "to condemn in judgment." Its synonym is *katakrsis*, which is "the process of judging that leads to condemnation." Therefore, there is now no katakrima for any Christian.

In view of that, Hebrews 9:27 is not addressing Christians. Verse 28 of Hebrews 9 says, "So Christ was so sacrificed once to take away the sins of many people; and he will appear a second time, not to bear sin, but to bring salvation to those who are waiting for him." If you study Hebrews 9 from verses 11 to 28, you will deduce that he was talking about Christ redeeming human creation from death into the eternal life.

Many Christians do not even know that they have the eternal life; they think we will live the eternal life when we get to heaven. John knew this; that's why he wrote to us in 1 John 5:13 to remind us that we have the eternal life now. Eternal life is the very nature of God, and we have that very life now. "Through these he has given us his very great and precious promises, so that through them you may participate in the divine nature" (2 Pet. 1:4). With the consciousness of the eternal life, you can look at death eyeball to eyeball fearlessly because you are not subject to death.

PART THREE

CHAPTER ONE

APOCALYPSE

The Revelation of Jesus Christ, which God gave unto him, to shew unto his servants things which must shortly come to pass; and he sent and signified it by his angel unto his servant John: Who bare record of the word of God, and of the testimony of Jesus Christ, and of all things that he saw. Blessed is he that readeth, and they that hear the words of this prophecy, and keep those things which are written therein: for the time is at hand.

—Revelation 1:2-3

THE AIM OF this part of the book is to teach the biblical report of the revelation of the end-time from the biblical context in order to avoid heresies and to deliver the cobelievers from the ignorance that heresies and a lack of understanding of the Word of God have put upon many of them. We must not forget that what Satan is really doing now is preventing Christians from the real knowledge of the Word of God so that they will live and die in ignorance.

The end-time events—starting from the destruction of the temple, the rapture of the saints, the appearance of the Antichrist, the seven-year holy covenant, the construction of the Jewish temple, the renewal of the daily sacrifice, the rise of the beast and false prophet, the mark of the beast (666), the great tribulations, the rise of the two sackcloth witnesses, the millennium, and the judgment—must not depart from our minds and always guide us in the expectation of the Master. Though there had been many predictions that predicted the end of the world, the predictions were actually according to scientific analyses and misinterpretations of the Word of God. But the sure way of getting the accurate timing of God for his program in the world is the Bible, and this book is helping to simplify what the Word of God says for your understanding so you will not live in the dark.

Actually, many of the prophecies of the end-time have been fulfilled; some are yet to be fulfilled, and we are living in the fulfillment of some because we are in the end-time era. The Antichrist may be alive somewhere today; the battle of Armageddon is drawing closer in the Middle East. The rapture of the church will soon take place because the holy covenant will be signed speedily; then all the events described in the book of Daniel and Revelation will take place.

JESUS'S PREDICTIONS

I have heard some set of folks saying that end-time events described in the Bible had happened already, that the rapture will not take place, and that there is nothing like the Second Coming of Jesus, but my studies tell me that they are ignorant of the Word of God. In the year 2002, I came across a history lecturer in Lagos, Nigeria, who argued that history showed that the expectation of the Second Coming of our Lord Jesus Christ is insignificant because all that the Bible talks about his Second Coming had happened already. At the end of his argument, he made it clear that his argument was taken from the book of Matthew 24. That several wars and rumors of wars had been recorded without the appearance of Jesus and the Antichrist, so the scripture is not trustworthy.

For the benefit of this study and the enlightenment of the believers, it will be very important for me to discuss Matthew 24 and reveal what it was talking about in its context.

MATTHEW 24:1-31

Jesus left the temple and was walking away when his disciples came to call his attention to its buildings. Do you see all these things? He asked? Tell you the truth, not one stone here will be left on another; every one will be thrown down.

As Jesus was sitting on the Mount of Olives, the disciples came to him privately. "I tell us" they said, "when will this happen and what will be the sign of your coming and of the end of the age? Jesus answered, "watch out that no one deceives you for many will come in my name, claiming, I am the Christ, and will deceive many. You will hear of wars and rumors of wars, but such thing must happen, but the end is still to come. Nation will rise against nation and kingdom against kingdom. There will be terminus and earthquakes in various places. All these are the beginning of birth pains. Then you will be handed over to be persecuted and put to death and you will be hated by all nations because of me. At that time many will turn away from the faith and will betray and hate each other, and deceive many people. Because of the increase of wickedness, the love of most will grow cold, but he who stands firm to the end will be saved. And this gospel of the kingdom will be preached in the whole world as a testimony to all nations, and then the end will come.

So when you see standing in the holy place' the abomination that causes desolation', spoken of through the prophet Daniel—let reader understand then let those who are in Judea flee to the mountains. Let no one on the root of his house go down to take anything out of his house. Let no one in the field go back to get his cloak. How dreadful it will be in those days for pregnant women and nursing mothers. Pray that your flight will not take place in winter or on the Sabbath. For then there will be great distress, unequaled from the beginning of the world until now and never to be equaled again. If those days had not been cut short, no one would survive, but for the sake if eh elect those say will be shortened. At that time anyone says to you, 'look here is the Christ' or there he is' do not believe it.

For false Christ and false prophets will appear and perform great signs and miracles to deceive even the elect if that were possible see, have old you ahead of time.

"So if anyone tells you, 'there he is, out in desert,' do not go out; or here he is, in the inner rooms; do not believe it. For as lighting that comes from the east is visible even in the west, so will be the coming of the son of man, whenever there is a carcass, there the vultures will gather. Immediately after the distress of those days 'the sun will be darkened, and the moon will not give its light; the stars will fall from the sky, and the heavenly bodies will be shaken. At that time the sign of the son of man will appear in the sky and all the nations of the earth will mourn. They will see the son of man coming on the clouds of the sky with power and great glory. And he will send his angels with a loud trumpet call, and they will gather his elect from the four winds from one end of the heavens to the other."

The proper study of this chapter (Matthew 24:1-31) can be traced from the questions of the disciples in verse 3 of Matthew chapter 24.

I.   When Will These Happen?
II. What Will Be the Sign of Your Coming?
III. And of the End of Age?

Jesus answered the questions respectively, and for proper clarifications and with the help of the Holy Ghost, I will make sure I deal with the questions from Jesus's point of view and by the direction of the Holy Ghost.

I. When Will These Happen?

The disciples asked this question because Jesus predicted the destruction of the temple when he said, "I tell you the truth, not one stone here will be left on another; no one will be left on another; every one will be thrown down" (Matt. 24:2).

Jesus dealt with this question in verses 15 to 22. The prophecy was fulfilled when the Roman army under General Titus destroyed the temple in AD 70. Titus led his soldiers to destroy Jerusalem and the temple of Solomon. Jesus knew that this would happen and was aware of how terrible the scenario would be; that is why he said, "Then let those who are in Judea flee to the mountain. Let no one on the roof of his house go down to take anything out of the house. Let no one in the field go back to get his cloak" (Matt. 24:16-18). Jerusalem was destroyed, and all the Jews in the city fled and scattered around the world. The temple was destroyed. They stole all the gold in the temple. Not one stone was left on another when they were done searching for the remaining gold that melted in the temple when the temple was set on fire.

The destruction of Jerusalem in AD 70 was the impending fall of Jerusalem; it was not the Second Coming of our Lord Jesus, but it was the days of judgment and sorrow for the Jews. Jesus gave ample warning to the disciples. He enjoined them to heed to his words and escape the city in advance of the destruction of the city and the temple.

Historical fact reveals that the early Christians fled Jerusalem and none of them perished when the destruction took place in AD 70. Many Jews died, and thousands of them scattered around the world. For many years after the attack, no Jew could enter Jerusalem.

Jesus said, "They will fall by the sword and will be taken as prisoners to all the nations. Jerusalem will be trampled on by one Gentiles until the time of the Gentiles are fulfilled" (Luke 21:24). Jerusalem was attacked, and they actually fell by the swords of the Roman army.

The attack lasted for months; the destruction was horrible beyond explanations. Thousands of Jews died of starvation. When Titus's army broke into the city of Jerusalem, they slaughtered the city's citizens and set the city ablaze. It was even recorded that the blood of the slaughtered Jews extinguished the terrible fire that was set on the city, including the temple building.

Historians recorded that about 1,100,000 Jews were killed and 97,000 Jews were taken as slaves to many nations while others fled. After several years of those horrible events, some Jews could only come near Jerusalem hill and mourn their loss while under fear and terror.

II. What Will Be the Sign of Your Coming?

The second question requested for the sign of the coming of our Lord Jesus in the sky, and Jesus attended to this question in verses 23 to 31. "Then if any man shall say unto you, Lo, here is Christ, or there; believe it not. For there shall arise false Christs, and false prophets, and shall shew great signs and wonders; insomuch that, if it were possible, they shall deceive the very elect. Behold, I have told you before. Wherefore if they shall say unto you, Behold, he is in the desert; go not forth: behold, he is in the secret chambers; believe it not. For as the lightning cometh out of the east, and shineth even unto the west; so shall also the coming of the Son of man be. For wheresoever the carcase is, there will the eagles be gathered together. Immediately after the tribulation of those days shall the sun be darkened, and the moon shall not give her light, and the stars shall fall from heaven, and the powers of the heavens shall be shaken: And then shall appear the sign of the Son of man in heaven: and then shall all the tribes of the earth mourn, and they shall see the Son of man coming in the clouds of heaven with power and great glory. And he shall send his angels with a great sound of a trumpet, and they shall gather together his elect from the four winds, from one end of heaven to the other."

Jesus revealed the issue of the false prophet and those that will come in the name of Jesus Christ. He declared that many will claim to be the Messiah, but he said people should not believe them because they are children and servants of Satan.

He said a false Christ and false prophets will perform great signs and miracles to deceive people, even the so-called elects if possible. Jesus made it clear that his coming will be obvious to the entire human creation. The coming of Jesus will be very glaring as a gathering of vultures around a carcass. By the time he appears in the sky, the dead in Christ will rise and meet him in the sky, then we Christians who are alive will join him in the sky while also having changed from mortal to immortal.

But it must be clearly noted that Jesus Christ will not come down to the earth at the rapture because the Bible says he will only come to gather us (the Christians) from the four corners of the earth. He will be in the sky, and we will ascend to him there.

However, this will happen almost at the end of time; the peace agreement would have been signed. First Thessalonians 5:2-3 says, "For yourselves know perfectly that the day of the Lord so cometh as a thief in the night. For when they shall say, Peace and safety; then sudden destruction cometh upon them, as travail upon a woman with child; and they shall not escape." This is a revelation of how Israel will have a peace agreement with the power to have a mutual relationship and not fight each other but help each other to fight their respective enemies.

III. And of the End of Age?

The last question was on the event of the end of this world. And Jesus answered this question in verses 4 to 14 in chapter 24. And Jesus answered and said unto them, "Take heed that no man deceive you. For many shall come in my name, saying, I am Christ; and shall deceive many. And ye shall hear of wars and rumours of wars: see that ye be not troubled: for all these things must come to pass, but the end is not yet. For nation shall rise against nation, and kingdom against kingdom: and there shall be famines, and pestilences, and earthquakes, in divers places. All these are the beginning of sorrows. Then shall they deliver you up to be afflicted, and shall kill you: and ye shall be hated of all nations for my name's sake. And then shall many be offended, and shall betray one another, and shall hate one another. And many false prophets shall rise, and shall deceive many. And because iniquity shall abound, the love of many shall wax cold. But he that shall endure unto the end, the same shall be saved. And this gospel of the kingdom shall be preached in all the world for a witness unto all nations; and then shall the end come."

In this report, the events of the end of the world will start immediately after the rapture of the saints. The Antichrist will claim to be anointed and proven to be the Messiah. Terrible things will happen; fearful things that had never happened since the creation of the universe will happen on this very earth after that. Satan will freely operate on the earth because the new creations would have been taken away, but his days will be shortened because of the elect.

Wickedness that can never be compared with any kind of wickedness in the history of the world will take place, and things like that will never happen in the universe again. I'd like to point out here that Jesus tells us in the above scripture that during this time, the good news—the message of the kingdom—will be preached all over the world, then the end will come, which means that the gospel will be preached till the last day of the existence of this planet earth. When you read about the report of the events that will take place during the great tribulation, you will discover that there will be a place for the ministry of reconciliation because many will still accept the lordship of our Lord Jesus Christ during the time of tribulation.

The issue of the end-time will be clearly discussed in this book. The above discussed are just brief explanations of Matthew

24 though that is not all about Matthew 24. But because we are still going to learn more about the end-time event in other chapters of this book, I have therefore decided not to go deeper in discussing Matthew 24 for now.

SIGNPOSTS TO THE END OF THE WORLD

Our Lord Jesus gave us important and unmistakable information about the end-time events. Though all the events that Jesus predicted are not immediate events that will usher in the end-time, they are the events that must take place as a preparation of the end-time, no matter how long the end may be. Jesus predicted these events over two thousand years ago; many of these events have happened, many are happening, and the remaining ones will still happen. They are the signposts to the end of this age.

These Jesus predictions were recorded in Matthew 24, Mark 13:1-37, and Luke 21:5-36.

Wars and Rumors of Wars:

Historians have recorded several wars and rumors of wars. It is not possible to search any history textbook without reading about wars. As a matter of fact, before and after Jesus Christ, thousands of wars were recorded all over the world. This is because men live to take advantage of each other. Warfare has been part of the world; war is synonymous to human existence. Some of the greatest wars that the world can never forget are the European Revolution, Russian Revolution, and the American War of Independence; the world will never forget the First and Second World Wars.

There were uncountable wars among African states. Wars between African states and European countries were significant to the hypothesis of the scriptures. There were wars between European states. There were wars between European states and some other developing countries. There were several wars in the Middle East.

Wars and rumors of wars are continuous because men live to play save, and there will be more wars before the end of the world because men are in search of selfish freedoms and revolutions. Competition is the strength of human beings. This leads to acrimony, which is the root of calamities all over the world.

However, all these wars are not waged in the form of open confrontation; many of them were waged diplomatically in the form of propaganda, economic sabotage, cold wars, etc., and the last war will be fought in Megiddo. The Bible calls it the battle of Armageddon.

The world power (like America under the dispensation of Bill Clinton) had tried to prevent many wars that could lead to the third world war, which is the end-time struggle. Bill Clinton took it upon himself—the responsibility of preaching peace all over the world.

That is great, but total peace cannot be accomplished because the Word of God must come to pass; thus, it is the responsibility of the church of our Lord Jesus Christ to start preparing for the rapture by winning the world for Christ more than ever. We have more jobs to do now than we have ever been doing because the time is short and more souls must be won. We have to save more people into the kingdom of God to escape the future tribulation. We are to prepare physically and spiritually; the church is obliged to evangelize the gospel and lead the unsaved entities to Christ.

Thus, the number of people that will suffer the terror of the end-time chaos will be limited since the church will not participate in the suffering of the end-time struggle. The wars and rumors of wars that the world is experiencing today are just like birthing pains. They are shadows of reality, and we are not supposed to be filled with the negative effects of the wars and rumors of wars no matter how terrible the effects of the wars may be because we are not of the world. The church has to be taught that we live by a different set of rules. Jesus said there will be wars and rumors in the world; that does not include us. We are not of the world; therefore, we are not supposed to feel what the rest of the world feels; we are a special, different set of beings.

The problem many Christians have is that they lack knowledge of the Word of God; they are very careless. That is why they meet themselves in the predicament they are in today. If the wisdom of God can guide you, you will live as the king that you are in this same, seemingly problematic world. Until the church comes to the knowledge of their purpose in life, they will have the same problem the world has.

A Christian is not supposed to be a victim of any circumstance; when men say there is a casting down, we have been ordained to say there is a lifting up. We do not have to complain like the unconverted because we are special. We are in the God class of being. We have the very life of God in us. We are not subject to the circumstances of this world. We have the Holy Ghost. No matter what happens at this perilous time, we are to stand strong always. We have been equipped by the Holy Ghost to dominate our spheres of contacts.

There will definitely be troubles in this world, but they are not for us or against us. Even when we are facing difficult times, we are sure of coming out strong because we have overcome the world in Christ Jesus. It is not actually compulsory for war to break out in the nation you live in before the rapture takes place. You can stop the escalation of any calamities in the country, state, or locality that you live in. Remember, you are the salt of the earth. You are the preserver of your world and everywhere you have contact with. This world is preserved because we are here. There will be an unspeakable free manifestation of the satanic activities if the Christians are not here.

Famines:

The number of chronically hungry folks in the developing and underdeveloped countries are extremely unspeakable. Most of the recorded wars had generated terrible levels of poverties and famines. France's revolution, for instance, broke out due to famines and hunger caused by the satanic nature of their king.

One of the aims and objectives of the League of Nations was to eradicate hunger, but the League of Nations failed to eradicate famines because some of its members were selfish, strong names who aggressively invaded small and weak nations. This eventually resulted to the Second World War. The United Nations also aims to eradicate poverty, but the result on the ground shows that poverty is growing in the developing and underdeveloped countries.

The World Health Organization reveals that over one billion folks sleep without food every night. Many people live on less than one dollar a day. The world population is increasing fast, and natural resources are diminishing rapidly. This is one of the causes of famine, and the greatest famine will still take place during the great tribulations.

Wide Spread of Iniquities:

As the coming of the Lord is getting nearer, iniquities will spread like never before. Government officials will rule and parade themselves in arrogance like the devil would do. They will talk rough and carelessly against people of God and his kingdom. That is what is going on all around the world. Immoral laws have been put in place in many nations. There have been several political and parliamentary bills and enacted laws to discredit the beauty of the gospel. Many nations set up regulations against the preaching of the Word of God. Same-sex marriage is approved in many countries. This is the devil obviously at work; the coming of the Lord is obviously around the corner. How can you explain the legalization of abortion, homosexuals, etc.? Some nation's financial policies have put the citizens under bondage; some underdeveloped countries adopted policies to take advantage of the citizens. Heavy taxes have been put on people without any reasonable return.

The spread of iniquities cannot be overemphasized. Just because human beings are functioning with the satanic nature, the nature of disobedience, they find it difficult to obey even the laws they set up by themselves. Crime is rampant in our societies; evil has been systematically legalized in many nations.

It was said by some folks that "let us do evil to achieve good." This is a satanic statement in the mouth of egocentric entities. It is a sign of the last day. The Antichrist will utter thousands of more terrible statements than this.

Earthquakes:

Many nations have been destroyed by several earthquakes. There is no year without report of earthquakes on the face of the earth. In the year 2005, there were records of earthquakes in Asia. In some other part of the world, the same had been experienced in the past. And the world will still experience the greatest one under the administration of the Antichrist.

Pestilence:

The World Health Organization (WHO) reports the discovery of new diseases in the different parts of the world. In spite of the national and global campaigns for health and against life-threatening diseases, a large percentage of the number of the world live on drugs as a result of increased diseases and their effects. Unfortunately, the already discovered viruses and diseases cannot be totally eradicated, and new ones are coming to existence. Life spans of men on the face of the earth are getting shorter day by day. HIV/AIDS is killing hundreds of millions of people every day, and more deadly diseases are being originated by the devil from the realm of darkness and are killing people. The devil is taking advantage of hundreds of millions of people all around the world, but we are not subject to all these. If you ever get sick, it is because you allow it; no sickness should fasten itself unto you because 1 Peter 2:24 says, "Who his own self bare our sins in his own body on the tree, that we, being dead to sins, should live unto righteousness: by whose stripes ye were healed." Every sin and sickness that existed, those existing now, and those sicknesses that will still be originated later have been laid on the cross and settled. Sickness and death can only fasten themselves on the sinners and die; they are not for you to use. What you have to do is to use your mouth to control your life. You have the onus to tell your body every day that "the life of God is in me"; "I will never be sick in my life"; "The divine life is in every fiber of my body"; "That life is in my blood, water, cells, and ligaments"; "No sickness can attack me in the name of Jesus." If you will say this to yourself every day and be conscious of that reality, no sickness or pestilence in the world can attack you.

Persecution and Killing of Christians:

Right from the day of Pentecost, believers have been facing unspeakable persecution. Many of them were imprisoned, and many were killed. This will highly increase as the world continues; there were increases on the number of persecuted Christians. Many Christians were killed by swords; some were crucified and destroyed. Some were beheaded. In these last days, the persecution does not just happen continuously, but it has increased and changed radically to political, military, economical, social, and technological persecution. Thousands of missionaries were killed for preaching Jesus and creating churches all around the world. Almost all the terrorist attacks all around the world are carried out by Islamic terrorist sects against the Christians, so every nation that has good populations of Christians will continue to be attacked by the deadly terrorists. The United States of America, Israel, and Nigeria have been hated and been attacked again and again because of the Christians. They hate us with passion unspeakable and are determined to stop our global growth and domination. They have mandates from the devil to destroy us, but we are indestructible.

False Prophets:

There were many false prophets in the last centuries, and they are increasing today because they are making big money through it today. Many claim to be prophets of God and persecute the real children of God. They launch attacks and persecutions against prophets of God. There was a period that a man called himself Jesus in Lagos, Nigeria. The level of religiosity is increasing in the world, and it is having a negative effect in our societies. They do this in preparation of the coming of the Antichrist. The real false prophet will still come during the great tribulations to work with the Antichrist.

The Love of Many Growing Cold:

The love of many Christians is growing cold because of what is happening all around the world. The Christian race is a love race as the Bible describes, but it is very difficult to find the real love of God among the so-called Christians; people are mostly self-centered. This is simply another sign of the coming of the Lord. Now, the world is full of confusion. Even many Christians suspect themselves; thus, they cannot live a love life among each other.

Because many are in search of security, they have run into unending calamities that do not allow many Christians to function in the love of God. As a matter of fact, many do not know what is called love toward God or a fellow believer because selfishness has lorded over average human beings.

Some Christians cannot confess the lordship of our Lord Jesus outside, particularly in the presence of unbelievers, because of the environment they find themselves in. Scripturally, love is expressed by faith because we are talking about unconditional love. It is the ability to love the unlovable. The nature of a Christian is a nature of love. If you function in love, you will preach the gospel because you will love the unsaved and want them saved.

Many prophecies in the Word of God reveal that this will take place when the end is at hand. Apostle Paul wrote that perilous times would come in the last days.

But mark this: There will be terrible time in the last days people will be lovers of themselves, lovers of money, boastful, proud, abusive, disobedient to their parents, ungrateful, unholy, without love, unforgiving, slanderous, without self-control, brutal, not lover of God, treacherous, rash, conceited, lovers of pleasure rather than lovers of God—having a form of godliness but denying its power. (see 2tim 3)

The Bible admonishes us not be naive because there are difficult times ahead when the end of time is at hand. He said that as the end approaches, people are going to be self-absorbed, corrupt, money-hungry, self-promoting, stuck-up, profane, contemptuous, crude, coarse, dog-eat-dog, unbending, slandering, impulsively wild, savage, cynical, treacherous, ruthless, bloated windbags who are addicted to lust and allergic to God. They'll make a show of religion, but behind the scenes, they are animals. Get this clear: if any of the above describe you, you are simply an animal subject to the devil. Please stay clear of these people (2 Tim. 3:1-5). In this world of God, we can see the level of evil in the world. It was predicted that evil will be increased rapidly.

This is the evening part of life. The day is getting dark; unconverted souls are in trouble. Everything is working against them, which is the reason the seemingly strong people are taking advantage of the weak strategically. In today's world, killings, riots, and wars are rampant; homosexuality is nothing to many. Civilization has been misunderstood and misused. These are the increasing wickedness in our societies. Happy are the new creations because we are the light of the world; though the world is in a financial crisis and the global economy is breaking down, the darker the day, the brighter the light. You have to be conscious of the truth that the Christians are not designed to function according to the standard and economy of the world. We have a special strategy in the kingdom of God. What you need to do is get deep into the Word of God, do the Word of God, and live beyond the standard of the world economy.

In the book of Nahum chapter 2 verse 4, the Bible renders a prophecy that "the chariots storm through the street, rushing back and forth through the squares. They look like flaming torches, they dart about like lighting." Civilization is good, but God said they will be part of the signs of the end-time. There are great and mind-blowing discoveries in the world today, but they are the mechanisms to draw the coming of the Master more rapidly. Another good example of the new-age discoveries that enhance the coming of the Master's coming is the technology with the aid of the Internet. The Internet is a great tool in the hand of God and the hand of the devil too. We preach the gospel online, and the devil also uses the Internet to deceive people too. Thus, the Internet and all other technologies are not necessarily tools of the devil for deception; the Internet and all other technological gadgets are also vessels for us to win people into the kingdom of God.

The increase in automobiles was prophesied to be a sign of the end-time; there was no automobile in the world when the prophet Nahum prophesied about a rapid increase in automobiles. That is why Nahum called it a chariot because chariots were what they had in the world then for mobility, but he noticed these chariots (automobiles) having features that made it look like flaming torches (i.e., the vehicle's light). The plan of God to increase automobiles in the world is to speed up the preparation for the coming of the King in a very short future.

In the book of Daniel chapter 12 verse 4, the Bible says, "But you, Daniel, close up and seal the words of the scroll until the time of the end. Many will go here and there to increase knowledge." Daniel prophesied that there would be an increase in traveling and searching of knowledge when the end is at hand. This is what must happen because it has been preprogrammed by God. Ninety percent of the third-world countries are potential travelers who increase the level of human knowledge in our societies. As the world's civilization improves every day, the means of transportation improves, then international traveling increases. The Word of God will travel more all around the world and win souls. The challenge is that the continuous search and acquisition of more human knowledge has been taken advantage of by the people of satanic influence to deceive the people and reduce the level of knowledge of God; this is a satanic means of causing more unbelief in the world. Remember, human knowledge is directly against the Word of God, but we have a better chance. We have the possession of the divine wisdom and knowledge of God; we can subdue the kingdom of Satan with the in-depth wisdom of God; after all, the whole world belongs to us.

CHAPTER TWO

THE END-TIME AND THE ISRAELITES

THERE IS NO way we can separate the end-time events from the Israelites or separate Israelites from the end-time event. The Israelites have to be our major focus in this study if we are really going to embark on any objective study about the end-time events. The Bible shows God's heartbeat for these specially elected people. Any study on the end-time events that does not consider the Israelites is in the risk of futility. The greatest events of the end-time have a direct connection with the nation of Israel. Many things that had happened to and through the Israelites speak loud about the end-time.

It has been recorded that Jerusalem was invaded and destroyed by the Roman soldiers under General Titus's command in AD 70. This event is highly significant among the events of the end-time because this is what scattered the Jews around the world and led many of them to prisons.

In AD 182, some Jews entered the city of Jerusalem secretly and dwelled in it; this is because there is no place like home. They have a passion for their nation, but fear of invasion still dominated them.

Christianity had some influence in Jerusalem for a little period of time before the Muslims under Omar took over the city AD

637. The Muslim movement took over in the city (Jerusalem) in AD 637; they built their temple (the Dome of the Rock) on the site of the destroyed temples. All these happened to prepare for the end-time events; all these took place in the Middle East. The AD 637 Muslim movement did not invade Jerusalem on an easy ground; they invaded the city by force and killed people that resisted their faith before they built their third most sacred mosque in the world, and the killings were continuous for a year before they gained an upper hand over the Jews; thus, the Israelites scattered all over the world.

The Israelites scattered among all nations; they experienced trouble for a very long period of time. But God did not abandon them completely; this is why they always dominated whoever they met. God always preserved and blessed them miraculously because they are the elect of God. He had selected them from the beginning to fulfill his plan. Due to the way God deals with them even in foreign lands, people always hate them so the Word of God may be fulfilled.

The Bible declared in the book of Jeremiah chapter 16 verses 14-15 about the Israelites: "However, the day are coming declares the Lord, when men will no longer say, As surely as the Lord Lives, who brought the Israelites up out of Egypt, but they will say; as surely as the lord lives, who brought the Israelites up out of the land of the north and out of all the countries where he had banished them. For I will restore them to the land I gave their forefather."

This prophecy was saying that the Israelites would not boast of their deliverance from the hand of the pharaoh in Egypt only; that the time is coming when they will be boastful of their restoration from the north and every part of the world—meaning many nations will take advantage and maltreat them, but God will always deliver them.

This prophecy started its fulfillment after the First World War; after the First World War, Adolph Hitler of Germany dealt with the Jews with the spirit of a nationalist. The Jews in Germany were killed; millions of them were executed with terrible capital punishments because God blessed them. They seemed to have dominated the German economy.

The entire world felt the Jews' pains greatly and sympathized with them. The United Nations voted to divide Palestine between the Arabs and the Jews while Jerusalem was to be their capital. But the Arabs rejected it with a preparation to wage war against Jews if they tried to step into the land. In May 14-15, 1948, Israel was declared a nation for the first time since the captivity of Babylon in 597 BC. These opened doors for wars in the Middle East between the Arabs and the Israelites; after this great event, there were several emigrations recorded in Israel, and Jews are still moving from many countries to Israel.

Luke 21:24 prophesied that Gentiles will control Jerusalem until the time of the Gentiles is fulfilled, and this prophecy was in effect from AD 70 to 1967 when the Israelites assumed the control of their capital city (Jerusalem). In the 1970 s and 1980s, numerous Jews left Russia for Israel. In 1984, about fifteen thousand Jews escaped starvation in Sudan; they actually fled to Israel. In 1991, about twenty thousand Jews fled to Israel from Ethiopia. These are the little that I can give in this book, but this does not mean that this is all about the movement of the Jews from the foreign countries to Israel because research shows that their immigration still continues, and it will be so until they are fully restored; no threat of war, terrorist attack, and religious opposition can stop them because the show tells us it will be so, and nothing can change it. Even if the whole world stands against them, they will still win. The Word of God cannot be defeated by any nation's principle and/or policy.

In Zephaniah 3:9, God said, "Then will I purify the lips of the people that all of them may call on the name of the Lord." Another translation renders the quotation as thus: "I will return to you a pure language." The Hebrew Language had become a dead language for a long time before now, but the Hebrew language has been restored back to the Israelites as an official language. This decision was made in 1982. At last, the forgotten and dead (Hebrew) language is effectively functioning as an official and national language in Israel. Zechariah 12:6 says, "On that day I will make the leaders of Judah like a firepot in a woodpile, like flaming torch among sheaves. They will consume right and left all the surrounding peoples, but Jerusalem will remain intact in her place."

The above prophecy is all about the future of the Israelites. He knew they will have enemies but assured their victories. God has been granting the Israelites military and political victories. There were several military and terrorist attacks that had been raised against them by the Arabs after 1948 till this date, but the Israelites always overcome them. This victory will surely continue till the end of the great tribulation.

UNBELIEF OF ISRAEL

The greatest of the Israelites' problems is the problem of unbelief. The Israelites were the first people to know about the first coming of Jesus. They knew the Messiah would come to save the world, but when Christ came, they could not recognize him. Instead of believing him, they killed him. Jesus knew this, which is why the Bible says, "Therefore speak I to them in parables: because they seeing see not; and hearing they hear not, neither do they understand. And in them is fulfilled the prophecy of Esaias, which saith, By hearing ye shall hear, and shall not understand; and seeing ye shall see, and shall not perceive: For this people's heart is waxed gross, and their ears are dull of hearing, and their eyes they have closed; lest at any time they should see with their eyes, and hear with their ears, and should understand with their heart, and should be converted, and I should heal them" (Matt. 13:13-15). Jesus said this because he knew that it had been said by the prophet and it must come to pass. Isaiah the prophet prophesied that the Israelites will open their eyes and see not; they would listen but understand not. This is the very reason they could not accept Jesus. Their hearts had become calloused. Instead of believing and accepting Jesus Christ as their Messiah, they are still waiting for him to come even when he was with them. They rejected salvation and held on to the law of sin and death that had been done away with in Christ Jesus. They pursue righteousness by work. Apostle Paul testified about these people when he said they were zealous for God but lacked knowledge (see Rom. 10:2). That is why God said, "My people are destroyed from lack of knowledge" (Hosea 4:6).

This does not mean that all Israelites rejected Christ, but many of them rejected him to fulfill the prophecy of God. Remember what God said about the Israelites in the Deuteronomy 32:21: "They made me jealous by what is no God and angered me with their worthless idols. I will make them envious by those who are not a people, I will make them angry by a nation that has not understanding." Christianity was forced out of Jerusalem by the Israelites when they started killing the apostles by capital punishment. Their rejection of Christ enhances the spread of the gospel on the face of the earth today. God can now be the father of anyone who believes.

One thing is expected of the Israelites for the fulfillment of the Word of God. They are to make Christ as the Lord of their heart. Zechariah 12:10 says, "And I will pour upon the house of David, and upon the inhabitants of Jerusalem, the spirit of grace and of supplications: and they shall look upon me whom they have pierced, and they shall mourn for him, as one mourneth for his only son, and shall be in bitterness for him, as one that is in bitterness for his firstborn," and I know this will be made possible by accepting Christ as the Messiah. Apostle Paul said that God did not reject his people (the Israelites). Therefore, it is clear that the Israelites will still turn to God at the appointed time because God himself said, "Yet I reserve seven thousand in Israel all whose knees have not bowed down to Baal and whose mouths have not kissed him" (Kings 19:18).

The seven thousand in the above scriptures is a symbolical number of the completeness of the divinely preserved godly remnant. It is clear that the scriptures talk about the reserved

Israelites that will turn to God at the late hour. That is why Apostle Paul said categorically that all Israelites will be saved (see Rom. 11:26), but this will happen toward the coming of the Lord Jesus.

PROJECTS OF THE JEWS

One of the most important projects for the Jews today is the rebuilding of the temple located on the Mount Mariah. But the presence of the Dome of the Rock, the third most sacred mosque in the world, is the obstacle of the Jews.

It has been clearly stipulated in this study that the temple of Solomon was destroyed in AD 70 by the Roman armies led by General Titus. Between AD 687 and 691, the Muslims later built their mosque at the site of the destroyed temple. The Muslims believed that Muhammed was taken up to heaven on that land. The taking of the temple by the Muslims is what God referred to in Revelation 11:2 when the Bible says, "But the court which is without the temple leave out, and measure it not; for it is given unto the Gentiles: and the holy city shall they tread under foot forty and two months." Gentiles are the people that are not of the Jewish nations. God knew this would happen long before it happened, and the record has been in the Word of God long before it ever happened because the event is very important to the coming of the Lord.

The Jews have a burning passion to rebuild that temple, and this will be made possible through their covenant with a European nation (i.e., the Antichrist). Immediately this starts; that means the great tribulation is about to start.

During the first and early period of the great tribulation, the mosque will be pulled down, and the Arab nations and Muslims all around the world will rise against the Jews, but they will defeat the Arabs and the rest of the Muslim world, and the temple will be freely built.

THE RAPTURE OF THE CHURCH

In a moment, in a twinkling of an eye, at the last trump: for the
trumpet shall sound, and the dead shall be raised incorruptible,
and we shall be changed.

—1 Corinthians 15:52

The word *rapture*, from the Greek word *harpazo*, means "to be caught up or taken away suddenly." The rapture refers to the sudden removal of all of God's people on the earth. In the twinkling of an eye, born-again Christians will suddenly be transformed out of our human bodies and will rise up into the air to join Jesus Christ. All Christians are expecting the rapture of the church; this is the reason we preach the gospel at every opportunity. We are eagerly expecting the coming of the Master in the sky; we love to be with the Master, but we have to do more than before to bring more people out of darkness and into the glorious light of the gospel.

But many people are misunderstanding the provision of the Word of God concerning the rapture. The reason is that the rapture has been presented to us as something mysterious; they make us think that the rapture will take place in a way that we will be definitely ignorant of it. The truth is that the rapture will take place soon and we will play more roles in bringing the rapture to its manifestation.

Israel is already playing its role in bringing the rapture of the church to its manifestation by making all efforts to rebuild the temple, which can only be possible through the peace that will be signed between Israel and a nation that will be headed by the Antichrist.

Daniel 9:26-27 says, "And after threescore and two weeks shall Messiah be cut off, but not for himself: and the people of the prince that shall come shall destroy the city and the sanctuary; and the end thereof shall be with a flood, and unto the end of the war desolations are determined. And he shall confirm the covenant with many for one week and in the midst of the week he shall cause the sacrifice and the oblation to cease, and for the overspreading of abominations he shall make it desolate, even until the consummation, and that determined shall be poured upon the desolate." The peace treaty will be signed, but we would have raptured before the treaty begins, and we will know when the time has fully come; we may not know the specific day, but the Holy Ghost in us will teach us all things because we are workers with him till the time.

It is true that the rapture will take place in a moment, in a twinkling of an eye. We have to know that we will rapture incorruptibly just like the dead. It means that the church of Jesus Christ has the responsibility of growing in Christ Jesus. We have to be faithful in the work of the Lord because we have a job of winning the world to him; that is our mandate.

If you are conscious of the fact that all things are of God, who has reconciled us to himself by Jesus Christ and has given us the ministry of reconciliation according to 2 Corinthians 5:19, you will not think about the sudden rapture of the church because you will know when it will take place.

If you study the scripture closely, we can come close to telling the world when the rapture will take place and warn them against the terror awaiting those that are not born again before they die or the rapture takes place. Hosea 6 gives more light about how close we are to the rapture of the church; really, Jesus will appear in the sky soon, and we will join him in the sky with the dead in Christ. We will rapture together, and it will meet the unregenerate ones in their ignorance like a thief in the night. It will take place in a very sudden manner to them, and they will have nothing to do about it because they failed to take advantage of our message; we are telling the unsaved ones to accept the lordship of Lord Jesus Christ.

PREDICTING THE TIME

In Hosea 6:1-2, God gives clues to when the rapture will take place. You have to be aware of the fact that the restoration of Israel will determine our rapture because we will not be here during their struggle with the Antichrist. The prophecy of Hosea, son of Beeri, in chapter 6:1-2 in the Bible says, "Come, let us return to the Lord. He has torn us to piece but he will heal us; he has injured us but he will bind us up our wounds. After two days he will revive us; on the third day he will restore us that we may live in his presence." The Message version of the Bible renders it as follows: "Come on, let's go back to God. He hurt us, but he'll heal us. He hit us hard, but he'll put us right again. In a couple of days we'll feel better. By the third day he'll have made us brand-new, Alive and on our feet, fit to face him."

This is wonderful. Israel has already gone astray. They had lost so much because of their disobedience to the Word of God. And many things around them are telling us that they are already calling on God for a rescue. God left them alone as they chose. They had been torn into pieces; millions of them were killed in different attacks. As they are now calling on God, he is reviving them in all ramifications. The prophecy tells us that their revival will be after two days, which took place in about the 1000s; a very good example is the establishment of the Israeli nation in 1941.

This is one of the events that took place in the 1000s (after the two days) as a sign of the reviving of Israel. "But do not forget this one thing, dear friends: with the Lord a day is like a thousand years" (2 Pet. 3:8). The Lord has revived the Israeli nation in the 1000s, and he is restoring them already; this is the third day, and he will restore them completely before the end of these 2000s. They will live in the presence of God. They will live with the church in the presence of God in the millennial kingdom in the third day, which is the middle of 2000s.

The truth is that the end will come before the 3000s because Israel will be restored on the third day, which is some time in the 2000s. The new creation and the surviving Jews will be in the millennial kingdom of Jesus on the third day some time before the end of the 2000s and after the great tribulation. And a specific period can even be hypothetically discovered if you can closely monitor the event that the Bible tells that will take place before the rapture of the church.

This is one of the best ways of knowing the time of the Master's coming. The understanding of the above scripture is an assurance of the fact that the Master will come before the end of this millennium. The rapture will take place before the end of this second millennium. Second Thessalonians 2:3 says, "Don't let anyone deceive you in any way, for that day will not come until the rebellion occurs and the man of lawlessness is revealed, the man doomed to destruction. He will oppose and exalt himself over everything that is called God or worshiped, so that he sets himself up in God's temple, proclaiming himself to be God." This is also enough to predict when the rapture will take place because it will be known when the man of lawlessness will come. The man of lawlessness is talking about the Antichrist; he will come like a nice man to help the people of God through the peace treaty, but he will betray and maltreat them. So when the peace is fully on, we will know how close we are to the coming of the Lord because we must rapture before the date of the ratification of the peace agreement.

"And now you know what is holding him back, so that he may be revealed at the proper time. For the secret of lawlessness is already at work; but the one who now holds it back will continue to do so till he is taken out of the way" (2 Thess. 2:6-7). The Antichrist will not come until we rapture to heaven. We are the ones holding back. That is the reason Jesus said that we are the light of the world. The Christians are the preservers of this planet. When his appointed time to be revealed comes, we will then be taken to heaven via the rapture before he comes. We are not in a hurry to go now because we still have so many souls to win; we have to be smart because the time is fast approaching. The coming of the Antichrist is not the major issue, but the restoration of Israel is, which the Antichrist has a major role to play. The time of the restoration of Israel is the time of the Antichrist, and we can see that the Israelites are working toward their restoration; therefore, all hands must be on deck.

I said that if you are in the Lord and you are serious about this matter, the rapture of the church will not be like a thief in the night to you because you will know the time. First Thessalonians 5:4 says, "But you, brothers, are not in the darkness so that this day should surprise you like a thief." The Bible only says that the rapture will be like a thief in the night to the world, not the new creations; after all, the job of the Holy Spirit is to tell us what happens in the kingdom of God. Why then does he have to keep this great information from us? That is why the Bible says that we are not in the darkness so that the coming of the Master will not be a surprise to us.

> After this I looked, and there before me was a door standing open in heaven. And the voice I had first heard speaking to me like a trumpet said, come up here and I will show you what must take place after this. (Rev. 4:1)

The rapture of the church is best explained in the book of Revelation; thus, I will focus the scope of this study on the book of Revelation though I may bring in some related scriptures that talk about our subject.

John was the last apostle that was facing persecution sometime around AD 95 after the destruction of Jerusalem and the temple. Also the killing and arrest of other apostles had taken place. John went to exile on the island of Patmos, and he was there as a Christian missionary. He received this revelation under terrible pains and suffering. Jesus visited him when he was praying and showed him many things about the seven churches and told him to write down all that he saw because Jesus wanted to show him what will happen in the future and therefore make him know how to prepare for the future.

In chapter 4 of the book of Revelation, God took John away to heaven. God changed their discussion from the present to the future. The event of the rapture is the call of the Lord when Jesus will appear in the air (see Thess. 4). The rapture of the church will take place at the immediate moment before the ratification of the treaty of peace between Israel and the European power. The rapture is for us who have accepted Christ and prepared for the coming of the Lord. The dead in Christ will first rapture and meet Jesus in the sky, then we who are on the earth (the believers) will then change from mortal to immortal and ascend to the sky to meet Jesus in the air. This is not the Second Coming of Jesus because he will not come down to the ground; he will only appear in the sky, and we will go join him in the sky and go to heaven together with Jesus for a period of seven years.

Jesus foretold to the disciples this in John 14 when he told them that he would go and prepare a place for them in heaven, and he said he will come back to take the saints after the preparation. We are going to be where Jesus is in heaven; that is why he said, "I will come back and take you to be with me that you also may be where I am" (John 14:3). The saints will be caught up with Christ, and the seven-year treaty of peace and friendship will take effect between Israel and a European champion by the Antichrist; the tribulation will start, then the end will come.

THE SEALS AND THE SCROLL

For the sake of this study, I will like to discuss the horrible events that will happen on earth during the great tribulations from the book of Revelation's view. "And I saw a mighty angel proclaiming in a loud voice, who is worthy to break the seals and open the scroll? Then one of the elder said to me. Do not weep! See, the lion of Judah, the Root of David, has triumphed. He is able to open the scroll and its seven seals" (Rev. 5:2,5).

The seals contain what must happen during the tribulation; there is no one worthy to open the seals. Only Jesus can open the first seals, as observed by John who was watching the events as a sprit. He said, "I looked and there before me was a white horse! Its rider held a bow and he was given a crown, and he rode out as conqueror bent on conquest" (Rev. 6:2).

This is the Antichrist riding on a white horse, holding a bow and with a crown on his head. This signifies his coming, pretending to be the Christ. The Antichrist is actually a false Christ. He will come claiming to be the Messiah who can give peace and deliver the world from its troubles and also help the children of God. He will present himself in an honorable way, and people will honor him because of what he will have in control.

The Antichrist will declare the new world order with strong economic, political, spiritual, and military power. He will use all that he will possess to deceive many, but God has given the absolute power and victory to Jesus. Jesus possesses the real crown of glory.

Jesus opened the second seal, and John saw a red horse; the rider was given the power to take peace from the earth and make man to kill each other, and he will be given a long sword. "And when he had opened the second seal, I heard the second beast say, come and see. And there went out another horse that was red: and power was given to him that sat thereon to take peace from the earth, and that they should kill one another: and there was given unto him a great sword" (Rev. 6:3-4).

This is a revelation of the great global war that will take place during the first three and one-half years of tribulations. The red horse symbolizes a bloody war that will take place when the Jews, with the support of the Antichrist, will pull down the Muslims' third sacred mosque (the Dome of the Rock) and build their intended temple. The Bible shows that the rider of the red horse will take away the peace of the earth as a sword was given to him. The Arab nation and the global Muslims will wage war with the Jews, but the Jews will conquer them with the support of the Antichrist. During the period of that war, multitudes of people will be killed, many nations will be destroyed, and many kingdoms will be brought to naught.

Jesus opened the third seal, and John saw a black horse! And its rider was holding a pair of scales in his hand. The black horse symbolizes a great famine. "And when he had opened the third seal, I heard the third beast say, Come and see. And I beheld, and lo a black horse; and he that sat on him had a pair of balances in his hand. And I heard a voice in the midst of the four beasts say, A measure of wheat for a penny, and three measures of barley for a penny; and see thou hurt not the oil and the wine" (Rev. 6:5-6).

This unfortunate scenario will be caused by the great war of tribulation. Many rich will become poor. Many business organizations will be destroyed. There will be terrible inflation that can never be controlled with any kind of economic policy. No economic policy will be able to control the inflation. It is only the olive oil and wine that would not be destroyed by the rider of the black horse. This may be because the roots of the olive go deeper and would not be easily attacked by the first drought.

Jesus opened the fourth seal, and John saw a pale horse! Its rider was named Death, and Hades was following close behind him. And they were given power to kill people by swords, famine, and plague. "And when he had opened the fourth seal, I heard the voice of the fourth beast say, Come and see. And I looked, and behold a pale horse: and his name that sat on him was Death, and Hell followed with him. And power was given unto them over the fourth part of the earth, to kill with sword, and with hunger, and with death, and with the beasts of the earth" (Rev. 6:7-8).

This is as a result of the war, famine, and epidemics. During the war and the famine, many people will die. Death will reign more than ever. Mortuaries and cemeteries will be filled up to the extent that there will be no place for the dead to be buried.

Jesus opened the fifth seal, and John saw the souls of those who had been slain under the altar. "And when he had opened the fifth seal, I saw under the altar the souls of them that were slain for the word of God, and for the testimony which they held: And they cried with a loud voice, saying, How long, O Lord, holy and true, dost thou not judge and avenge our blood on them that dwell on the earth? And white robes were given unto every one of them; and it was said unto them, that they should rest yet for a little season, until their fellow servants also and their brethren, that should be killed as they were, should be fulfilled" (Rev. 6:9-11).

That altar is in heaven. The souls under the altar are the souls of the people who maintained their testimony of the Word of God during the tribulation. Though this set of people failed to rapture with the church because they were not born again, but immediately after the rapture, they will repent for their sins and embrace God. The gospels we are preaching today became their reference point, and they will confess Jesus as their lord and savior. They will not accept the mark of the beast and the mark of the Antichrist.

These people will be alive for the responsibility of warning people against accepting the mark of the beast though the Antichrist may not allow the Bible to be carried on the streets because the Bible talks about that people will be terribly dealt with, but this is still in God's testimony. Millions of them will be killed because of the acceptance of the lordship of our Lord Jesus. The Bible says that their souls will be under the altar in heaven during the tribulation because they will die like sacrifices offered to God. The people will weep bitterly and ask God to avenge their blood. This shows that even after the rapture, God will still save many people if they will repent.

Jesus opened the sixth seal; great, horrible things will happen naturally. There will be a great earthquake. "And I beheld when he had opened the sixth seal, and, lo, there was a great earthquake; and the sun became black as sackcloth of hair, and the moon became as blood; And the stars of heaven fell unto the earth, even as a fig tree casteth her untimely figs, when she is shaken of a mighty wind. And the heaven departed as a scroll when it is rolled together; and every mountain and island were moved out of their places. And the kings of the earth, and the great men, and the rich men, and the chief captains, and the mighty men, and every bondman, and every free man, hid themselves in the dens and in the rocks of the mountains; And said to the mountains and rocks, Fall on us, and hide us from the face of him that sitteth on the throne, and from the wrath of the Lamb: For the great day of his wrath is come; and who shall be able to stand?" (Rev. 6:12-17).

Nature will participate in the fight of the great tribulation. Nature will fight the earth. The sun will turn black. The moon will turn to something like blood, and the stars will fall to the earth. Mountains will be removed. Fearful things will happen; men will hide themselves under mountains, but no mountain will be capable to hide them from the wrath of the greatest ones. Men will look for rescue, but they will not find one.

Before the opening of the seventh seal, God will send four angels to stand at the four corners of the earth to prevent any wind from blowing on the earth. God will do this to stop the problem of the earth and prevent wars on the earth for some time. The wind that the angels will prevent from blowing on the earth signifies a temporary suspension of war. Thus, there will be no war and killing on the earth for a specific period of time; this will be done by God to do his work of salvation. You have to be aware of the fact that soul winning is the number one business of God. The temporary suspension of chaos on the face of the earth will be judiciously used by God to win many people to his kingdom. Though the time will be very short, it will be highly productive.

God will send another angel; he (the angel) will tell the four angels who will be given power to harm the earth not to harm the earth until a seal is put on the forehead of God's servants. God will give him power to seal 144,000 people from the tribes of Israel. It is very obvious that God the Father himself will not come to this earth to preach the gospel; he will definitely use his servants. I have to say this at this junction that the Greek word that was used for *angel* here can also mean *messenger*, and I am of the opinion that God will not use angels to preach the gospel but human beings. The gospel is given to human beings to preach, not angels. No angel will preach the gospel, and none will preach it at the time of tribulation. Every Christian is a potential soul winner, so we are his angels—his messengers. Therefore, if you ever come across something that talks about an angel sent by God to preach the gospel, just be aware that the word is *messenger* and it is talking about the man preaching the gospel during the tribulation.

CHAPTER THREE

THE GREAT TRIBULATION

A CCORDING TO THE Word of our Lord Jesus Christ, the phrase "great tribulation" refers to the last half of the tribulation. In Matthew 24:21, Jesus said, "For then there will be a great tribulation, such as has not occurred since the beginning of the world until now, nor ever shall." This is the period that is referred to as the manifestation of the abomination of desolation; the man is the Antichrist.

Some may argue on how we are really sure that the tribulation will last seven years. The answer can be found in Daniel 9:24-27 and Revelation 11:1-2.

> Seventy weeks are determined upon thy people and upon thy holy city, to finish the transgression, and to make an end of sins, and to make reconciliation for iniquity, and to bring in everlasting righteousness, and to seal up the vision and prophecy, and to anoint the most Holy. Know therefore and understand, that from the going forth of the commandment to restore and to build Jerusalem unto the Messiah the Prince shall be seven weeks, and threescore and two weeks: the street shall be built again, and the wall, even in troublous times. And after threescore and two weeks shall Messiah be cut off, but not for himself: and the people of the prince that shall

come shall destroy the city and the sanctuary; and the end thereof shall be with a flood, and unto the end of the war desolations are determined. And he shall confirm the covenant with many for one week: and in the midst of the week he shall cause the sacrifice and the oblation to cease, and for the overspreading of abominations he shall make it desolate, even until the consummation, and that determined shall be poured upon the desolate.

The prophecy foretold a period of seven times seventy yet to come or seventy-seven-year periods. Seventy-seven-year periods equal to 490 years because biblically, one week is referred to as seven years; definitely, seventy weeks means 490 years. Therefore, the above prophecy was saying that 490 years has been determined by God. After the transgression of sin would finish, wickedness will end and the righteousness of God will reign for every prophecy of God will be completely fulfilled. And the anointed one (Jesus Christ) will come and reign as king of the world.

In 605 BC, Babylon took the Jews captive and destroyed the city of Jerusalem. God then told Prophet Daniel during his prayer that the Jews would be restored back home and Jerusalem will stand until the anointed one (i.e., Jesus Christ) comes. God told Daniel that this would happen in seven weeks and sixty-two weeks (i.e., sixty-nine weeks).

In March 14 of 445 BC, King Artaxerxes of Persia approved the restoration of Jerusalem, and some of the Jews that were taken captive to Babylon returned back to Jerusalem.

In April 6 of AD 32 (i.e., sixty-nine weeks or 483 years after), the anointed one (i.e., Jesus Christ) entered Jerusalem on a donkey (see Matt. 21:1-11). After these, sixty-nine weeks have passed already. It remains just only one week, which is seven years. In verse 27 of chapter 9 of the book of Daniel, it was declared that the remaining one week (i.e., seven years) will be fulfilled during the period of the Antichrist. He will set himself up in the temple of God. The prophecy declared that this will be confirmed as a covenant under the remaining one week (i.e., seven years). God also prophesied that this will happen until the end (i.e., the one week that remains will also determine the end of the world). Therefore, the great tribulation will last one week, which means seven years biblically.

The scripture reveals that the events of the last week (seven years) are preprogrammed by God as the event that must take place at the end of the age. The Antichrist will be the major actor (empowered by Satan) in the event of the last (final) age.

His coming and reign will not be a matter of sudden or unexpected occurrence; it will rather be a well-prepared and preprogrammed event. We must be very careful not to mistake the Antichrist for Satan. The Antichrist is not Satan, and he will not be Satan; he is going to be a man like you and me, but he will be a man of great influence with powerful socioeconomic and political power.

The Antichrist will be the president of the *new world order*. The new world order is the description of a period of time in the very near future that will change the world's political thought and the unity of power. It is the concept of global governance with an initial aim of addressing worldwide political and economic problems.

He can simply be referred to as the world president because he will champion the world other. It is obvious that the world is in an economic mess now as a result of the recession. But he will bring about temporary socioeconomic and political stability in the world. He will bring about socioeconomic, political, educational, and religious reform all over the world, which will be acceptable and efficacious for the period of his reign. In terms of peace, there would be peace; there will be a series of peace treaties and alliances. He will be a diplomatic and deceitful man that will not be easily predicted. Satan will use him to draw people's attentions to his false generosity. Many nations will come under his socioeconomic and political influence; they will love him for his deceitful good deeds.

Though, for the proper fulfillment of the Word of God, many nations will believe in him and have a direct relationship with him. He will have ratified his relationship with the Jews based on the signed peace treaty (agreement); that agreement will be for socioeconomic, political, and military support from him, but in the middle of the seven years (which is the three and one-half years), he will break the peace agreement. He will stop sacrificing and offering to God in the temple. He will enter the most holy place and sit in the most holy place in the temple. He will demand for the sacrifice and offerings that are supposed to be offered to God. He will call himself God. He will remind them all of the socioeconomic, political, and military support he had given to them. Though the Jews will resist him, they will not be able to overpower him easily. This is what will cause the outbreak of war.

The reign of the Antichrist in the temple and his entering of the most holy place is what the Bible refers to as the abomination of desolation because it is an abomination for any man that is not a high priest to enter into the most holy place; equally, no gentile must enter into the most holy place. The first abomination took place when the Roman soldiers, led by Titus, entered the temple, took all the gold in the most holy place, destroyed the temple, and set it on fire.

REVELATION 11:1-2—THE OUTER COURT

> I was given a rod like a measuring rod and was told God and measure the temple of god and altar, and count the worshipers there. But exclude the outer court; do not measure it, because it has been given to the Gentiles. They will trample on the holy city for 42 months.

The outer court that God asked John not to measure is the location that the Muslims built the Dome of the Rock on; that is why God said it had been given to the Gentiles (i.e., it had been given to the nations that are not Jewish nations). God then chose this scripture to express the struggle that will take place between the Jews and the Arab nations before the mosque will be pulled down and before the rebuilding of the temple, and God as well indicates that this struggle will last forty-two months, which is 3.5 or three and one-half years. And these three and one-half years is the first part of the seven years of the great tribulations.

THE FALL OF THE GREAT BABYLON AND MARRIAGE SUPPER

> And after these things I saw another angel come down from heaven, having great power; and the earth was lightened with his glory. And he cried mightily with a strong voice, saying, Babylon the great is fallen, is fallen, and is become the habitation of devils, and the hold of every foul spirit, and a cage of every unclean and hateful bird. For all nations have drunk of the wine of the wrath of her fornication, and the kings of the earth have committed fornication with her, and the merchants of the earth are waxed rich through the abundance of her delicacies. And I heard another voice from heaven, saying, Come out of her, my people, that ye be not partakers of her sins, and that ye receive not of her plagues. For her sins have reached unto heaven, and God hath remembered her iniquities. Reward her even as she rewarded you, and double unto her double according to her works: in the cup which she hath filled fill to her double. How much she hath glorified herself, and lived deliciously, so much torment and sorrow give her: for she saith in her heart, I sit a queen, and am no widow, and shall see no sorrow. Therefore shall her plagues come in one day, death, and mourning, and famine; and she shall be utterly burned with fire: for strong is the Lord God who judgeth her. (Rev. 18:1-8)

Babylon is a description of the kingdom that the Antichrist will rule. It will be wrong to call one country as the Babylon. Babylon is a description of a lawless nation where the kingdom of the Antichrist will be established. Some people have erroneously said that America will be the Babylon, but the truth is that there is nowhere in the Bible referring to America as the Babylon. In fact, I have personally searched the role of America in the world during the tribulations, but I cannot find any scripture that talks about the role of America in the tribulation. However, the Antichrist will not come from America; the scripture is very clear about this. The Word of God shows that the Antichrist will come from Europe, and the specific nation where he will come from in Europe will be revealed in this book as you continue reading.

Thus, Babylon is not talking about a particular nation as a geographical location but a system based on satanic sociopolitical, religious, and economic ideologies. Babylon the Great will become the citadel of evil because the Antichrist will dwell there and all demonic power will have direct influence on the people of that city; it will be the capital of the Antichrist. Every nation that will disobey God will be under the influence of the Antichrist, and they will have a relationship with Babylon the Great.

The Antichrist will function with his political, economical, and military power and tabernacle in Babylon. But Babylon will be destroyed by the great earthquake and atomic bomb; that city of sin will be destroyed by both natural and mechanical disasters. Because it is the place that always rejects God and encourages other nations to disobey God politically, economically, and spiritually, God will punish her inhabitants in his righteousness.

The wrath of God will come upon the city of the Antichrist; the great Babylon will be burned to ashes during the wars. All other kingdoms that have a political and economic relationship with the Antichrist will mourn and cry bitterly for him. All nations who have an economic relationship with him through trading will also weep bitterly for his destruction. All saints, apostles, and prophets in heaven will rejoice over the destruction of Babylon; the final pronouncement will be made on Babylon by God, and it will not be able to rise again. This will be done to avenge all the evil that had been done in that city and the killing of prophets and saints that had taken place in that city (see Rev. 18:1-24).

After the fall of the great Babylon, there will be praise in heaven; God will be praised for his great judgment. There will be shouting of "Hallelujah"; smoke that will signify victory will go up in heaven forever and ever. The twenty elders and the four living creatures in heaven will bow and worship God. After all these, the marriage supper of the Lamb will be announced with a voice of glory that will sound like a great multitude and like the roar of rushing waters.

After our being taken up into heaven, God will reward us based on the fulfillment of God's purpose in our respective lives. We that receive salvation through grace are not going to receive rewards for that, but we are going to receive rewards for working in the vineyard of God as ambassadors (Rev. 2 and 2 Cor. 5:20). The Bible says, "Let us celebrate, let us rejoice, let us give him the glory! The Marriage of the Lamb has come; his Wife has made herself ready. She was given a bridal gown of bright and shining linen. The linen is the righteousness of the saints" (Rev. 19:7-8, MSG).

During the marriage supper of the Lord, we will be given fine linen; bright and clean to wear this is to signify our righteousness by faith. It's only we who are born again, the virgins of God—the church that Jesus is waiting for; Jesus is our husband. "The Angel said to me, 'Write this: "Blessed are those invited to the Wedding Supper of the Lamb."' He added, 'These are the true words of God!'" (Rev. 19:9, MSG).

The Old Testament saints like Abraham, Moses, Joshua, Jacob, John the Baptist, and all the people that will come out of the tribulation will be blessed for witnessing the marriage supper of the Lamb. Think about it: if those who will witness the marriage supper will be blessed, how blessed are we, the wives of the Lamb?

144,000 SEALED: REVELATION 7

The number 144,000 has been misinterpreted by many people; the Jehovah's witnesses claim that it's only those 144,000 people who will go to heaven. This had misled millions of people all over the world. This has made people not to see reason for

Christianity because they have erroneously been made to believe that the number of people that will rapture is already complete.

The Bible makes it clear that the 144,000 people are the tribes of Israel that have been preserved by God. They are the faithful remnant. God will use these 144,000 to gain many souls during the tribulation. God started the reaching out to people from the Jews and will end it with the Jews; indeed, they are God's people.

They will preach the gospel of our Lord Jesus Christ; they will sacrifice their lives and save uncountable people from all the nations of the earth. God will give the great multitude that will be saved through their white robes. They will all be in white robes and hold palm branches, standing before the throne of God with praise in their mouths as a sign of victory and gratitude to the Almighty God.

The people that will be saved from the tribulation will not sit on the throne with us; they will not put on crowns. They will not receive rewards like we that believe and accept in Christ Jesus by faith because they are not products of the rapture, but they will be very happy to have escaped from the tribulation without the mark of the beast. That is why they will praise God with the palm branches that signify victory.

In verse 5 of Revelation 7, God gave us the comprehensive list of the tribes of Israel that will be sealed.

From the tribe of Judah, 12,000 will be sealed.
From the tribe of Reuben, 12,000
From the tribe of Gad, 12,000
From the tribe of Asher, 12,000
From the tribe of Naphtali, 12,000
From the tribe of Manasseh, 12,000
From the tribe of Simeon, 12,000
From the tribe of Levi, 12,000
From the tribe of Issachar, 12,000
From the tribe of Zebulun, 12,000
From the tribe of Joseph, 12,000
From the tribe of Benjamin, 12,000

The tribe of Judah came before Reuben in that list because Christ came from that tribe of Judah. The name of Dan was omitted from the list because the Danites set up for themselves idols in the book of Judges; it was written, "And the children of Dan set up the graven image: and Jonathan, the son of Gershom, the son of Manasseh, he and his sons were priests to the tribe of Dan until the day of the captivity of the land" (Judg. 18:30).

And Manasseh, one of the two Joseph tribes, was stipulated instead in place of the Danites. The seal that is being talking about here is the Holy Ghost. God will put the seal of the Holy Ghost on the children of Israel as a sign of ownership just as he put the same seal upon us. Everyone that believes and accepts the lordship of Jesus Christ has the seal of the Holy Ghost on them. This seal is what will empower and embolden them for the work of the ministry because it is setting them apart to preach the gospel to the rest of the world because it is impossible to preach the Word of God without the Holy Ghost.

THE SEVENTH SEAL

And when he had opened the seventh seal, there was silence in heaven about the space of half an hour. And I saw the seven angels which stood before God; and to them were given seven trumpets.

—Revelation 8:1-2.

When the seventh seal is open, there will be silence in heaven for about half an hour; this is an opportunity given to the people on earth to repent and come to God through the preacher on the face of the earth. After that opportunity, John saw seven trumpets. The sound of the each of these trumpets will bring about God's judgment on the people of the earth. The sound of the trumpets will determine the kind of calamities that will happen on the face of the earth.

The first angel will sound his trumpet; immediately there will be hail and fire mixed with blood. A third of the earth will be burned. "The first angel sounded, and there followed hail and fire mingled with blood, and they were cast upon the earth: and the third part of trees was burnt up, and all green grass was burnt up" (Rev. 8:7, KJV).

This will happen during the first three and one-half years of the tribulation. The hail and fire mixed with blood talk about the release and effects of nuclear bombs. This is a terrible modern weapon of war. The release of several nuclear bombs will destroy one-third of the human beings, one-third of the trees, and one-third of the living creatures of the earth.

Today, many countries have already made nuclear bombs; the question is, what do they want to use it for? These are the weapons prepared for the war during the great tribulation. I pity those that do not believe in the gospel because it will be too late for them to realize that this gospel is real. The fact is that the gospel is believable because these are real. If there will not be destruction on the earth, why then are the nations building weapons that can destroy the earth?

The second angel will sound his trumpet; something like a huge mountain all ablaze will drop on the sea, and all the seas will turn into blood, and all the living creatures in the ships will be destroyed. What will drop on the sea like a huge mountain are several nuclear bombs that many nations will send against each other, and they will destroy one-third of the creatures in the sea and ships.

The third angel will sound his trumpet, and a great star, blazing like a torch, will fall from the sky to the one-third of the rivers and on the springs of waters. The name of the star is Wormwood. Thus, one-third of the waters will be bitter, and many people will die as a result of that. "And the second angel sounded, and as it were a great mountain burning with fire was cast into the sea: and the third part of the sea became blood; And the third part of the creatures which were in the sea, and had life, died; and the third part of the ships were destroyed" (Rev. 8:8-9, KJV).

The above-mentioned star does not mean the stars in the sky; it is referred to as stars because it landed on the rivers, blazing like a torch. "And the third angel sounded, and there fell a great star from heaven, burning as it were a lamp, and it fell upon the third part of the rivers, and upon the fountains of waters; And the name of the star is called Wormwood: and the third part of the waters became wormwood; and many men died of the waters, because they were made bitter" (Rev. 8:10-11, KJV). These are actually biological bombs that will contaminate one-third of the rivers and one-third of the springs of waters. The bombs will make the water bitter, and they will have terrible effects on the water to the extent that those that will drink it will die.

The fourth angel will sound his trumpet; a third of the sun will be struck. A third of the moon and a third of the day will be without light; a third of the night will bring no light as well. "And the fourth angel sounded, and the third part of the sun was smitten, and the third part of the moon, and the third part of the stars; so as the third part of them was darkened, and the day shone not for a third part of it, and the night likewise" (Rev. 8:12, KJV). This is a result of the nuclear war.

When the third of all the trees, ships, and lands are destroyed, the dust and smoke from the explosions will cover the earth terribly, and everywhere will be darkened; the intensity of the dust will be so great that the dust will be stuck on the face of the earth.

Can you imagine how terrible the smoke of the burned houses, trees, human beings, etc., will be? We are all aware that it's Russia, Syria, or Iran against Israel. The Middle East simmers toward a boiling point, and a US, British, and Israeli intelligence monitors closely Iran's mission for a nuclear bomb that might even be used against America. Millions of Christians, Jews, Muslims, and even secularists are becoming more intolerant; thus, I really don't think anyone should doubt the reality of the prophecy of the Word of God about the end-time because of these events all around the world.

The sound of the fifth trumpet will be more terrible than the first four. Thus, God will authorize an eagle to declare three woes to the earth because of the trumpet that will be sounded. By the time the fifth angel sounds the fifth trumpet, a star that had fallen from the sky to the earth will appear. The star is said to have been given the key to shut off the abyss. He will open the abyss, and then smoke will rise from it; the smoke will be great to the extent of covering the sun and sky. Thus, the opening of the abyss will be full force.

The Bible says locusts will come down to the earth. The locusts will be given power like that of scorpions. They will be authorized not to harm the grass or any plant or tree of the earth, but they will be authorized to harm those who do not have the seal of God on their foreheads—meaning that it is only the sealed twelve tribes of Israel and their converts that will not be harmed. The locusts here are talking about evil spirits that afflict the people of that age; there will be extreme cases of demon possessions, and the people will not be able to do anything about them. It is very possible that the evil spirits will want to afflict the people with the Holy Ghost, but they will be able to rebuke them, and they will surely flee.

The 144,000 sealed Israelites and their converts will not be harmed by the locusts because they must have learned how to rebuke the devils, but all other human being on the earth will be harmed.

A STAR FROM ABYSS

The fifth angel sounded his trumpet, and I saw a star that had fallen from the sky to the earth. The star was given the key to the shaft of the Abyss. When he opened the Abyss, smoke rose from it like the smoke from a gigantic furnace. The sun and sky were darkened by the smoke from the Abyss. And out of the smoke locusts came down upon the earth and were given power like that of scorpions of the earth. They were told not to harm the grass of the earth or any plant or tree, but only those people who did not have the seal of God on their foreheads.

They were not given power to kill them, but only to torture them for five months. And the agony they suffered was like that of the sting of a scorpion when it strikes a man. During those days men will seek death, but will not find it; they will long to die, but death will elude them. The locusts looked like horses prepared for battle. On their heads they wore something like crowns of gold, and their faces resembled human faces. Their hair was like women's hair, and their teeth were like lions' teeth. They had breastplates like breastplates of iron, and the sound of their wings was like the thundering of many horses and chariots rushing into battle. They had tails and stings like scorpions, and in their tails they had power to torment people for five months. They had as king over them the angel of the Abyss, whose name in Hebrew is Abaddon, and in Greek, Apollyon. (Rev. 9:1-11, NIV)

The star that will come out of the abyss is Satan. He is the one that was given the key of the bottomless pit, where evil spirits are imprisoned. He is the king of the hell. They will harm the unsealed people; the people will like to die in order to end their pain and agony, but they will not be able die. The devil will have death taken from them because he will really want them to suffer the agony to bring glory to himself. It has been preprogrammed by the devil that nobody will die as a result of the poison power given to the locusts, but the harmed people will suffer pains terribly. The locusts are the demons that will come with the devil from hell. They will possess and afflict the people on the face of the earth.

The sixth angel will sound his trumpet; he will be asked to release the four angels who are bound at the great river Euphrates, and the four angels who had been kept ready for that terrible day will be released to kill one-third of mankind. "One woe is past; and, behold, there come two woes more hereafter. And the sixth angel sounded, and I heard a voice from the four horns of the golden altar which is before God, Saying to the sixth angel which had the trumpet, Loose the four angels which are bound in the great river Euphrates. And the four angels were loosed, which were prepared for an hour, and a day, and a month, and a year, for to slay the third part of men" (Rev. 9:13-15).

These are actually messengers of death; they are not angelic beings. They are called angels because the Greek word *angelos* was used to describe them in the original manuscript. The number of the mounted troops will be two hundred million. Many countries are building their armies strongly. And it is very certain that an army of two hundred million will be gathered; this will be the beginning of the battle of Armageddon.

Before the sound of seventh trumpet, many things will happen both in heaven and in the earth that will be discussed in this book, but I would like to discuss one of the events that will happen before the sound of the seventh trumpet, and that is the coming of the two witnesses.

THE TWO WITNESSES

> And I will give power unto my two witnesses, and they shall prophesy a thousand two hundred and threescore days, clothed in sackcloth. These are the two olive trees, and the two candlesticks standing before the God of the earth.

> And if any man will hurt them, fire proceedeth out of their mouth, and devoureth their enemies: and if any man will hurt them, he must in this manner be killed. These have power to shut heaven that it rain not in the days of their prophecy: and have power over waters to turn them to blood, and to smite the earth with all plagues, as often as they will. And when they shall have finished their testimony, the beast that ascendeth out of the bottomless pit shall make war against them, and shall overcome them, and kill them. (Rev. 11:3-7, KJV)

At this time, the first three and one-half years of the tribulation must have been far fast spent; many things have changed, and the world would have come under the second three and one-half years of the great tribulation. This period can be referred to as the second part of the great tribulation; the Antichrist would have broken the treaty between him and the Israelites. He would have set up his image in the newly built temple. He would have started revealing his real personality in full force. The whole world must pay back what he had falsely fully given to them.

Before the sound of the seventh trumpet, God will give power to two witnesses to preach the gospel to the people that will remain on the face of the earth because some of them will be saved.

These two witnesses will be fashioned after Moses and Elijah. It could be directly said that these two witnesses are Moses and Elijah because of their backgrounds and other scriptural information about both of them (respectively). Malachi 4:5-6 says, "See, I will send you the prophet Elijah before that great and dreadful day of the Lord comes. He will turn the hearts of the fathers to their children, and the hearts of the children to their fathers; or else I will come and strike the land with a curse." This scripture shows that Elijah is one of the two witnesses; he will come before the prophesied day of the Lord.

Revelation 11:6 says that these men have the power to shut up the sky so that it will not rain during the time they are ministering. According to the Word of God, we know that when the Israelites disobeyed God and worshipped idols during the reign of King Ahab, Elijah prayed to God that it might not rain, and it did not rain for three and one-half years.

"Now Elijah the Tishbite, from Tishbe in Gilead, said to Ahab, 'As the Lord, the God of Israel, lives, whom I serve, there will neither be dew nor rain in the next few years except at my word'" (1 Kings 17:1). Elijah was a man just like us. He prayed earnestly that it would not rain, and it did not rain on the land for three and a half years (James 5:17). This spiritual ability was given to Elijah to shut the sky, and he will do the same thing during the second three and one-half years of the tribulation.

God said that they will have power to turn the waters into blood and to strike the earth with every kind of plague as often as they want. When God wanted to use Moses to lead the Israelites out of Egypt, God gave him ten plagues to persuade the pharaoh in order to release the Israelites, and we can deduce that one of the ten plagues was the changing of water of the river Nile to blood. This same plague will be used during the second three and one-half years of the great tribulation.

Revelation 11:4 tells us that the two witnesses are the "two lamp stands that stand before the Lord of the earth." This is talking about the Lord Jesus Christ. In Matthew 17:1-13, Mark 9:2-13, and Luke 9:28-36, there were reports of transfigurations of Jesus Christ when Jesus took Peter, James, and John up a high mountain where he was transfigured with his clothes turning very white.

Moses and Elijah appeared to Jesus and had a nice communication with Jesus; this shows that Moses and Elijah had some mission in common. They also have a mission in the future that even relates to our Lord Jesus. Elijah did not see death, and God did not allow any man to see the body of Moses after his death; in fact, nobody was there when he died. This shows that God had something great in mind to accomplish through these people in the future; that is why he kept their bodies.

Some folks say that one of the witnesses is Enoch because he was translated. But that is not scriptural because he was not a Jew as he lived before the ministry of Noah. The two witnesses need to be "olive trees," and the olive tree represents the Jews. He does not fulfill any of the prophecies because he does not seem to have any of the spiritual abilities to do all that the witnesses will do.

"And the seven lamp stands are the seven churches" (Rev. 1:20). "These are the two olive trees and the two lamp stands that stand before the Lord of the earth" (Rev. 11:4). Though the lampstands represent the church, that does not mean that the witnesses are not Elijah and Moses; it only tells that the saints that were set free from the bosom of Abraham are now members of our family.

Every man that dies still lives in the eternity, but their bodies have been destroyed in the grave. But Moses's body was kept by God, which shows that his body is in a safe hand.

Moses and Elijah will come during the last part of the great tribulation in sackcloth. They will minister the gospel for about three years.

The ministry of the witnesses (Moses and Elijah) will be collective, and the ministry will be directly against the activities of the Antichrist. They will preach the salvation of God through faith in Christ Jesus. They will proclaim the death and resurrection of our Lord Jesus. They will reveal to the people that the Antichrist is not the Messiah. They will refer to the Antichrist as the prophesied false Christ. They will proclaim that the day of the judgment of God is at hand, and as a result of their message, multitudes will come to the knowledge of Christ and be born again.

This will terribly annoy the Antichrist and his forces; they will rise against the two witnesses. They will seek to kill them, but they will not be able to kill them until God's appointed time for them.

After the completion of the two witnesses' ministry, which will last 1,260 days, the Antichrist and his forces will attack them and kill them. He will throw their bodies into the street of Jerusalem—the place that is spiritually called Sodom and Egypt.

Their bodies will be on the street of Jerusalem for three and one-half days; people from different nations will come and look at their bodies on the street, and people will take pleasure in watching their bodies on the street. Jerusalem, because of the Antichrist, will not allow them to be buried; people will celebrate their deaths because the Antichrist will make people believe that they are false prophets. But after the three and a half days, a breath of life from God will be ministered to them, and they will stand on their feet and ascend to heaven.

Immediately there will be severe earthquakes; the whole world will be in terror and fear. There will be a voice calling them from heaven. The intensity of the earthquake will destroy a tenth of the city of Jerusalem, and seven thousand people will die in the incident. This will make the remaining people on the earth to be terrified and give glory to God (see Rev. 11:3-15).

The seventh angel will sound his trumpet after this; since the end is fast approaching, Jesus will be declared as the king of the kingdom of the world, and he must reign in it forever. Jesus is to reign in Zion. During the second three and one-half years of the great tribulation, a beast will come out of the sea with ten horns and seven heads and ten crowns on his ten horns. On each head, there will be blasphemous names.

THE BEAST

This prophecy is clearly related to the vision of Daniel. The beast that will come out of the sea is the head of the restored Roman Empire, which is the Antichrist. The sea that the Bible is talking about is a multitude of people; actually, the sea in the context of this scripture is the Mediterranean Sea, which means that the Antichrist will originate from the coastal region of the Mediterranean.

Historically, this location is the former territory of the Roman Empire. The proper elucidation of this is in relation to the coming of the Antichrist out of the (multitude) European kingdoms. He will be the leader of the European Union. This is the coming of the restored Roman Empire with strong economical, political, spiritual, and military power.

Due to the great contribution of the Antichrist to the world, nations will love him and be ready to work with him; this is because of all that he possesses. The national borders of the entire world will be eradicated, and the world will be divided into ten political zones. The world will be under one dictatorship—the Antichrist.

The Antichrist will be voted as the head of the world union, and Babylon will be the headquarters of the world union. Each political zone will have representatives in the world union. The Antichrist will enjoy global support from the world leaders. The Bible says that the beast will have ten crowns, and these ten crowns are the ten political zones under the world union. The ten political zones will have blasphemous names. The beast is said to have seven horns; these are the seven kingdoms that will stand against God and anything that has to do with God.

By that time, the Antichrist must have stopped the worship in the newly built temple in Jerusalem and demanded people to worship him; this will be the fulfillment of the desolation. It will be the period of the great abomination. Revelation 17:10 reveals that out of the several heads are the kingdoms of one body, and five out of the seven kingdoms are fallen; one is, and the last (one) kingdom is yet to come. In my search, I stumbled on a fact that says that the five kingdoms that have fallen are the following: Babylon, Egypt, Assyria, Medo-Persia, and Greece—the only kingdom that is on the ground today. Rome and the seventh kingdom that is yet to come is the world union that will be under the dictatorship of the Antichrist, and it is very clear that the world union will last for forty-two months, which is three and one-half years.

Babylon is a great city, one of the most important in the whole world, and this great city is made up of multitudes of different ethnicities. The seven heads are seven sequential kingdoms, and the ten horns are ten kings.

The great city is the main city of the eighth kingdom. John was told that five of those kingdoms had already fallen and the sixth one was the reigning kingdom at the time. The seventh kingdom had not yet come, and the beast itself was considered as an eighth kingdom that came out of the seven kingdoms.

At the time John saw the vision, the reigning kingdom was the Roman Empire; that is the sixth kingdom.

From the Bible's Daniel 7 and other historical records, we can find that the kingdoms are the following:

First kingdom—Assyrian Empire (Ezekiel 31)
Second kingdom—Egyptian Empire
Third kingdom—Babylonian Empire (612 BC-539 BC)
Fourth kingdom—Medo-Persian Empire (539 BC-330 BC)
Fifth kingdom—Greek Empire (330 BC-163 BC)
Sixth kingdom—Roman Empire
    West (31 BC-AD 476)
    East (31 BC-AD 1453)
Seventh kingdom—Ottoman Empire (AD 1299-AD 1922)

The Antichrist will be very powerful in his reign; he will destroy any man that stands against his rule with his spiritual and military power. In his broadcasts or reports on the television and radio and his addresses with the press, he will speak blasphemous things against God. Like never before, public relations activities will be magnified in the affairs of the world, but it will be perfected with spins and propagandas.

The dragon that was cast out of heaven (Satan) will give his power to the beast and his throne. This reveals that Satan will give power, authority, and a throne to the Antichrist to be able to function appropriately. The sources of the Antichrist's power will directly come from the devil. This does not mean that Satan will come out physically, but he will empower the Antichrist spiritually.

As the saga continues, the Antichrist will be attacked; he will be terribly wounded and killed, but his wounds will be healed, and he will be revived back from the dead magically. That will be the counterfeit and false imitation of the resurrection of our Lord Jesus. This is one of tricks he will use to deceive many people. The Bible says that the whole world will be astonished; due to that, many people will follow him and worship him.

MARK OF THE BEAST

> And the third angel followed them, saying with a loud voice, if any man worship the beast and his image, and receive his mark in his forehead, or in his hand. (Rev. 14:9, KJV)

The Antichrist will grow in political, military, and economic power; he will make the people of the world worship Satan because he (Satan) is the source of the Antichrist's power. The Antichrist will utter proud words to blaspheme against God, and he will be worshiped by all the inhabitants of the earth.

The Antichrist will gain all the power that will be needed to function against God; he will put the people of the world under his control. He will therefore introduce a new economic decree to control the economy of the world. He will ask every individual to receive the number 666 on their right hands or their foreheads as identities of his kingdom. They will force the people to receive the mark for economic purposes.

This mark is an agreement seal with Satan. The mark 666 is a number of imperfections that confirm the damnation of Satan, the Antichrist, the false prophet, and their followers. The number 666 is for the evil trinity: the satanic number is 6, the Antichrist's number is 6, and the false prophet's number is 6. Therefore, the mark 666 represents the evil trinity of wickedness. God will do everything to persuade people not to receive the mark, but many will be forced to receive the mark (see Rev. 13).

The angels that the Bible is talking about are the time-anointed and brave ministers of the gospel. They are actually human beings; we have to realize that the ministry of reconciliation is given to the converted humans, not angels; God is a god of order; he will not break the rules. The only source of people's misconceptions is because the scripture uses the Greek word *angelos*, which means *messenger*, for both angels and ministers that were to preach the gospel.

After the introduction of the mark 666 by the Antichrist, God will send three ministers to preach the gospel; they will announce the fall of Babylon and warn people not to receive the mark of the beast and persuade them not to worship the beast and his image. The three angels will preach the gospel to the whole world and announce the fall of Babylon to mark the end of the world.

There shall come two folds of harvests. The Bible declares, "I looked and there before me was a white cloud and seated on the cloud was one like a son of man with a crown of gold on his head and a sharp sickle in his hand. Then another angel came out of the temple and called in a loud voice to him who was sitting on the cloud 'take your sickle and reap, because the time to reap has come, for the harvest of the earth is ripe'" (Rev. 14:14-15).

A son of man, here is Jesus Christ on the white cloud and with a golden crown. This shows that Jesus is a king. He will harvest people that have sober minds and repented during the last period of the second three and one-half years of the tribulation. This is the harvest of the remaining martyrs. These will be the last set of people to come to Jesus. They will believe the gospel preached by the angels and be saved.

The second harvest is the gathering of the unbelievers and the proclamation of the wrath of God on them; after the proclamation of the wrath of God on the unbelievers on the face of the earth, God will release another wrath on the earth through seven angels with seven last plagues. Immediately germs will destroy the bodies of every individual who received the mark 666. Their bodies will be ugly and sticking; there will be terrible sores on their bodies.

The second angel will pour out his bowl on the sea, and the sea will turn to blood; the water will be like the blood of dead men, and every living creature in the sea will die. The third angel will pour out his bowl on the rivers and springs of water, and they will become blood; people will suffer from thirst because there will be no drinkable water.

The fourth angel will pour out his bowl on the sun; this will increase the heat of the sun like fire and kill many people.

The fifth angel will pour out his bowl on the throne of the Antichrist; this will cause other calamites even in the kingdom of the Antichrist. There will be great darkness around him, and chaos will be the result of this; instead of them repenting for their evils ways, they will grow in wickedness. The Antichrist will make them believe that the occurrences are just coincidental natural catastrophes.

The sixth angel will pour out his bowl on the great river Euphrates, and its water will dry up to prepare the way for the kings from the east. The great river Euphrates will dry up to eradicate the borders of east and west for the preparation for the battle of Armageddon.

When the river of Euphrates is eradicated, the evil spirits will instigate all the kings of the whole world to gather for the battle of Armageddon. The fact is that the nations from the east will be the major opponent of the Antichrist's global administration; they will not accept his global leadership. They would have a series of attacks from each other, but the miraculous drying of the river Euphrates will enhance the last global confrontation in Megiddo; that will be the final world war.

The seventh angel will pour out his bowl into the air and outside of the temple, and a loud voice will say "It is done" from heaven; there will be flashes of lightning, rumbling peals of thunder, and severe earthquakes. One of its kind since the creation of man, Jerusalem will split into three parts. The larger part of the world will collapse. And the wrath of God will come greatly on the great Babylon, and it will be destroyed (see Rev. 16:1-19).

CHAPTER FOUR

THE BATTLE OF ARMAGEDDON

And the sixth angel poured out his vial upon the great river Euphrates; and the water thereof was dried up, that the way of the kings of the east might be prepared. And I saw three unclean spirits like frogs come out of the mouth of the dragon, and out of the mouth of the beast, and out of the mouth of the false prophet. For they are the spirits of devils, working miracles, which go forth unto the kings of the earth and of the whole world, to gather them to the battle of that great day of God Almighty. Behold, I come as a thief. Blessed is he that watcheth, and keepeth his garments, lest he walk naked, and they see his shame. And he gathered them together into a place called in the Hebrew tongue Armageddon.

—Revelation 16:12-16 (KJV)

THE MESSAGE VERSION of the scriptures renders the scripture in a very simple way; it says, "The sixth Angel poured his bowl on the great Euphrates River: It dried up to nothing. The dry riverbed became a fine roadbed for the kings from the East. From the mouths of the Dragon, the Beast, and the False Prophet I saw three foul demons crawl out—they looked like frogs. These are demon spirits performing signs. They're after the kings of the whole world to get them gathered for battle on the Great Day of God, the Sovereign-Strong. 'Keep watch! I come unannounced, like a thief. You're blessed if, awake and dressed, you're ready for me. Too bad if you're found running through the streets, naked and ashamed.' The frog-demons gathered the kings together at the place called in Hebrew Armageddon" (Rev. 16:12-16, MSG).

The Word of God mentions the word *Armageddon* only one time in the book of Revelation. The original word from the Bible is *Ar Magedon*, which literally means "mount of Megiddo"—a city from which only ancient ruins remain. The ruins are located in northern Israel by the Kishon River on the southern edge of the plain of Esdraelon south of Haifa. This area seems to be where the battle of Armageddon will take place in the future as prophesied in the book of Revelation.

The battle of Armageddon is one of the crucial events that must take place during the second three and one-half years of the great tribulation. This is why the battleground was prepared for the showdown. The great river Euphrates that demarcated the east and west will miraculously dry up to enhance the movement of the east and the west for the battle of Armageddon. The battleground called Armageddon is at present called Megiddo; this is the place where the battle will take place. During the battle of Armageddon, the Chinese armies will oppose the armies of the Antichrist in Megiddo.

SECOND COMING OF JESUS AND THE MILLENNIAL

While the battle of Armageddon is going on, Jesus will come down from heaven; there will be a great shout from heaven. The coming of Jesus during the rapture is not what the Bible called the Second Coming of Jesus with us (the saints). Immediately the entire army of both the Antichrist and his opponent will collide under the leadership of the Antichrist. They will wage war against Jesus and the saints. But Jesus will capture the Antichrist and the false prophet, who will always perform the miraculous signs on behalf of the Antichrist. They will be thrown into the fiery lake of burning sulfur. Jesus will gather all the army and all the individuals and nations who received the mark 666 together, and they will be killed by the word that will come like a sword out of his mouth.

Those who do not receive the mark of the Antichrist and have no intimate relationship with him will survive the tribulation. All nations that did not accept the new world order will survive the tribulation and enter the millennial kingdom with Jesus and the saints, but they will not be in the same place with us (the church).

During the battle of Armageddon, the Bible declares that Jesus will come down from heaven to the earth. The entire army of the world, both the Antichrist's army and the opponents' army, will unite together to fight Jesus Christ on his coming. But my great Lord, the Lord Jesus, will capture the Antichrist and the false prophet (who will work together with the Antichrist) and throw them into the lake of fire. All the entities that have the mark 666 will be killed by the sword that will come out of Jesus.

In Revelation 20:1, the Bible says, "And I saw on an angel coming down out of heaven, having the key to the Abyss and holding in his hand a great chain. He seized the dragon, that ancient serpent, which is the devil, or Satan, and bound him for a thousand years. He threw him into the Abyss, and locked and sealed it over him, to prevent him from deceiving the nations any more until the thousand years were ended. After that he must be set free for a short time."

It could be asked, since the Antichrist and the false prophet have been thrown into the lake of fire, what will be the judgment of Satan who has been deceiving the whole world and giving power to the Antichrist? Well, Satan must be judged because he deceived them and led them to their chaotic situation.

God will send an angel to the earth with the key to the abyss. God will also give him a great chain to bind Satan. Satan will be burdened and thrown into the abyss (that is the middle of hell). Remember, the abyss is what God used to separate Hades and Geenna. The abyss is a place of confinement for evil spirits and Satan. He (Satan) will be bound with a great chain and locked up for a thousand years. Satan will not be thrown into the lake of fire with the Antichrist immediately after the tribulation, but he will be bound and seized in a great chain of pain and darkness in the abyss.

During this period, the great tribulation would have ended; the world will be free of sin and all acts of sin. The tempter, the deceiver, will be bound and seized in the abyss; therefore, no sin will be committed during this period.

The millennial kingdom is not going to be enjoyed by the saints and Jesus only but also by those that will survive the tribulations—those that will not receive the mark of the beast and did not die during and before the great tribulation. Jesus will be the head of the millennial kingdom. He will rule over the saints on this very earth. The Jews and people of other nations who survived the tribulation will enter the millennial kingdom with us though they will not enjoy all that we are going to enjoy, but they will still be happy for escaping the judgment that will be pronounced on the people who received the mark of the beast.

By the time we enter the millennial kingdom with all the other entities who did not receive the mark of the beast, those who have been killed because of their testimony for Jesus and refusal to worship the Antichrist will come to live and reign with Christ for a thousand years.

John said, "I saw thrones on which were seated those who had been given authority to judge" (Rev. 20:4). This shows that aside the throne of our Lord Jesus, there will be many thrones; these are the saints' thrones. The saints will be given power and authority to judge the unbelievers and wicked ones. The world will be populated again; people will live in peace and harmony. There will be no fights and war; nobody will sicken or die till the end of the one thousand years.

THE GREAT AND FINAL JUDGMENT

I saw an Angel descending out of Heaven. He carried the key to the Abyss and a chain—a huge chain. He grabbed the Dragon, that old Snake—the very Devil, Satan himself!—chained him up for a thousand years, dumped him into the Abyss, slammed it shut and sealed it tight. No more trouble out of him, deceiving the nations—until the thousand years are up. After that he has to be let loose briefly.

I saw thrones. Those put in charge of judgment sat on the thrones. I also saw the souls of those beheaded because of their witness to Jesus and the Word of God, who refused to worship either the Beast or his image, refused to take his mark on forehead or hand—they lived and reigned with Christ for a thousand years! The rest of the dead did not live until the thousand years were up. This is the first resurrection—and those involved most blessed, most holy.

There will be no second death for them! They're priests of God and Christ; they'll reign with him a thousand years. When the thousand years are up, Satan will be let loose from his cell, and will launch again his old work of deceiving the nations, searching out victims in every nook and cranny of earth, even Gog and Magog! He'll talk them into going to war and will gather a huge army, millions strong.

They'll stream across the earth, surround and lay siege to the camp of God's holy people, the Beloved City. They'll no sooner get there than fire will pour out of Heaven and burn them up. The Devil who deceived them will be hurled into Lake Fire and Brimstone, joining the Beast and False Prophet, the three in torment around the clock for ages without end. (Rev. 20:1-10, MSG)

The main period is about to take place at the end of the millennial kingdom. Satan will be released from the abyss, and he will be allowed to deceive the nations of the four corners of the earth. Satan will use this opportunity with desperation to get more people to his side because he knows that it will be his only chance to deceive them and gather people from the face of the earth once again. Satan will use that medium with great zeal to mobilize people against God's will.

This will be the last of Satan's rebellions against God. Satan will be smart enough to deceive many people among those who will enjoy the reign with Jesus and his saints during the millennium. God will use this medium to test the people who entered the millennium with us because they did not receive the mark of the beast. Just because there will be no sickness and death, the world will be rapidly populated during the millennial kingdom, but their faith has to be tested; that is why Satan will come to deceive many of them.

Satan will tempt them diplomatically; he will describe his imprisonment as injustice. He will deceive them with lies. Many of the people that will escape the tribulation will follow him, and a large percentage of the newly born entities that have never experienced the temptation of Satan before will also follow him because they will sympathize with him and follow him. Satan will coordinate and influence them to disobey God. Satan will gather them against God.

God refers to this evil gathering as Gog and Magog because the nations of the world will be together by Satan for a final assault on God. The Bible declares that the numbers of the people who will follow Satan will be like the sand of the sea.

God will judge them by sending down fire from heaven to devour them. Before this, the world will be divided into two groups. God's people will be in God's jurisdiction, and the deceived ones will be in the camp of the enemy of God. God will destroy the people who will go outside of God's jurisdiction with fire that will come down from heaven. Satan, who deceives them, will be thrown into the lake of fire where the Antichrist and the false prophet have been thrown. The three of them will be tormented in the lake of fire day and night forever and ever.

God will finally judge the entire universe, starting from the angels to all the human beings who had ever lived on the face of the earth, excluding the church. We (the church) are not going to be judged because Jesus was judged on our behalf on the cross and we were declared free (of judgment). There is no condemnation for us who are in Christ Jesus. As a matter of fact, we are going to judge the angels. The Bible says, "The day is coming when the world is going to stand before a jury made up of Christians. If someday you are going to rule on the world's fate, wouldn't it be a good idea to practice on some of these smaller cases? Why, we're even going to judge angels!" (1 Cor. 6:2-3, MSG).

The white throne of Jesus Christ will appear; the earth and the sky will roll up like a scroll to reveal the holiness of the white throne of judgment. The throne will be set up in the midst of the universe. The sky and earth will not be found; there will be no place for both the sky and the earth again.

All the dead—great and small, white and ebony, slim and fat, tall and short—will rise and stand before the great white throne, ready for the final judgment. All the dead in the sea and in hell will come out to be judged. God will not just throw them into the lake of fire. He will judge them legally. God will open several books that contain the deeds of every one of the human creatures. They will be judged according to what they have done as recorded in the books. The respective deeds of every one of them will be pointed out for proper clarification; thus, there will be no hiding place for anybody.

Really, there is no biblical, justifiable information that proves that anybody will be thrown to the lake of fire as a result of their wrong deeds. The only thing that God will throw the unsaved into the lake of fire for is the fact of their rejection of the lordship of Jesus.

Every human person that has ever come to this world has their name written in the book of life. But the name of everyone that is not born again will be blotted out of the book when they die without accepting Christ before death. At the final judgment and after the opening of several books, the book of life will open, and any name that is not found written in that book (the book of life) will be thrown into the lake of fire. God will open the book of life to show the judged ones that their names had been blotted out of the book of life as a result of their rejection of Jesus.

The absence of their names in the book of life shows that they are totally separated from the citizenship of God. They will be cast into the lake of fire; hell itself will be cast into the lake of fire. Death will be the last enemy to be thrown into the lake of fire. That is the second death and final judgment. That will be the end of sin and struggle; that time must be the primary focus of the new creation.

THE NEW JERUSALEM

And I saw a new heaven and a new earth: for the first heaven and the first earth were passed away; and there was no more sea. And I John saw the holy city, new Jerusalem, coming down from God out of heaven, prepared as a bride adorned for her husband. And I heard a great voice out of heaven saying, Behold, the tabernacle of God is with men, and he will dwell with them, and they shall be his people, and God himself shall be with them, and be their God. And God shall wipe away all tears from their eyes; and there shall be no more death, neither sorrow, nor crying, neither shall there be any more pain: for the former things are passed away.

—Revelation 21:1-4

After the final judgment, the present heavens and the earth will pass away; there will be no sea again. Old things will pass away to make room for a new heaven and a new earth. "Behold, I will create new earth. The former things will not be remembered nor will they come to mind" (Isa. 65:17).

A new heaven and a new earth will come into being; the New Jerusalem will come down from the new heaven. The New

Jerusalem will be the capital of the new heaven and the new earth. The New Jerusalem will be the dwelling place of God, and the saints will live with God in the New Jerusalem. The New Jerusalem will be too beautiful—beyond human descriptions; God will live with us there.

There will be no death, mourning, sorrow, or pain in the new heaven and earth. The New Jerusalem will be a great source of joy to God; he will delight in the saints that will live with him in the New Jerusalem. "'As the new heavens and the earth that I make will endure before me;' declare the Lord, 'so will your name and descendants endure'" (Isa. 66:22). God will enjoy the new heaven and new earth because it will bring everlasting joy to God's kingdom, so also will the saints enjoy the beauty and glory of the city because it will ensure our everlasting rest.

There would be no sea in the new earth; the climatic atmosphere and living condition will transform to God's new design of perfection. The glory of the New Jerusalem will not be compared with any glory. The city will have twelve gates, and twelve angels will stand at the gates respectively. The names of the twelve tribes of Israel will be written on the gates.

The names of the apostles will be written on the wall of the foundation of New Jerusalem. There will be a holy temple in the New Jerusalem where God and Jesus will dwell. The 144,000 sealed Jews and the church will dwell in the city with God and Jesus Christ. The righteous people that lived before Jesus will live and reign with us. Those who will be saved during the tribulation and who will survive the last temptation of Satan after the millennial kingdom will live in the new earth, but we (the new creation) shall be like Jesus in the New Jerusalem. This is the description of the Holy Ghost. The ministry of the Spirit will continue in the eternity.

From the throne of God and Jesus, there will be a flowing of the river of life down to the middle of the great street of the New Jerusalem; on both sides of the river of life, there will be trees of life bearing twelve crops of fruits that will be yielding its fruit every month.

This is the fulfillment of everlasting righteousness. There will be everlasting righteousness, and the glory of God will dominate the universe. And we shall be like angels, in a sense, but we are better than all angelic beings because they were created to serve us. We will partake of the mighty glory of God. Jesus will govern the world; he is the King of kings indeed. He is the king and ruler of the New Jerusalem. That is the kingdom of heaven. God will put everything under Jesus's authority. The New Jerusalem will be the exact manifestation of the glory of God. The beauty of the New Jerusalem cannot be compared with any kind of beauty in the world. The Bible records that the holy city will shine with the glory of God, and its brilliance will be like jasper, clear as crystal in the presence of John in his revelation. The wall will be made of jasper, and the city will be of pure gold as pure as glass. The foundation of the city will be decorated with every kind of precious item; the city will not require any external light. In fact, natural light like the moon or sun will not be there because Jesus will be the automatic light of the holy city. When God had seen the human generation fall in the Garden of Eden, what he immediately planned was this. All the dispensations, from the dispensation of innocence to the dispensation of eternity, are for the purpose of the New Jerusalem.

Jesus came and saved the whole world because of the New Jerusalem. God cannot afford the whole world to continue under the jurisdiction of Satan, and he cannot as well put men with their satanic nature into the New Jerusalem. Thus, the new creation came into existence by being born again; you and I are the purpose for the New Jerusalem. The New Jerusalem is the real place. It is the nation of Zionists. If you have any loved ones that are not yet born again, you better let them know what God has in store for them in the New Jerusalem; in case it is you (the reader) that is not born again, you better be born again now by confessing the following words and believing and meaning them with all your heart.

"Lord Jesus, I believe that you died and resurrected for me. I come to you today in the name of Jesus. I ask you to come into my heart to be the lord of my life. I receive eternal life into my spirit. I declare that I am saved. I am born again. I am a child of God. The greater one dwells in me right now. I am born again."

THE CITY OF GOD

The Bible shows that the new creation dwells in Zion right now. We also know that the new creation is the primary purpose of God for creating the earth. We are his real people. God wants to live among his children, the new creation, forever. The reason God will take us to heaven by rapture is because he does not want us at the tribulations when the Antichrist will reign in this very earth for the period of seven years. After the tribulations, we will come to understand that the new creation and those that will escape the tribulation without the mark 666 will reign with Jesus for a thousand years. After which, there will be eternity for the body of Christ. At the end of the millennial kingdom and final judgment, there will be the new heaven and the new earth.

The fact is that there will be no heaven separated from the earth. There will be heaven in the earth and earth in the heaven. Both of them will be in each other. What I am saying is that there will be Zion—where the entire membership of the family of God that are in heaven and we that are on earth right now will live forever in. Right now, all the members of the body of Christ live in Zion by faith in the spirit realm. But by that time, we will physically live in Zion. The present heavens and the earth will be done away with. We will not need faith to live in Zion; it will be as real as the present particle world is to us.

Now are we the sons of God; we are now in Zion. We were in there. This is our domicile. We are now in the city of God, our land of nativity. We believe and live our lives by this information because we have faith in the Word of God. God and many saints, including Jesus, are in heaven while we are here on earth with the Holy Ghost, and we are still functioning together as a family. This is greater, but the greater one will be here soon when the entire family will live together in a city. The saying of the scripture says,

"Now the dwelling of God is with men, and he will live with them" (Rev. 21:3).

Zion is the major plan of God. The Bible says that there shall be no sick people in Zion. The verse 4 of Revelation chapter 21 says that there will be no death, mourning, crying, or pain in the city of God for the old order of life has passed away. The new creation, in the face of death, requires faith to subdue pain, sickness, disadvantages, and death. The new creations that fail to do that in faith are always at the mercy of pain, sickness, disadvantages, and death. But in the new heaven and the new earth, we will require no faith to subdue the entire negative scenario because the devil will have been put where he belongs.

The Holy Ghost will be in Zion; we will still have the Holy Ghost in ourselves when we get there. Verse 6 of Revelation 21 says that to him that is thirsting, he will give drink from the spring of the water of life. No sinner will be there because what qualifies us to live in Zion is the eternal. At this time, all that are not born again will be in their place of damnation in the lake of fire out of Zion; there will be perfection of beauty.

Zion will be characterized with inexpressible divinity. We will be identified with God. God the Father and Jesus will be at the temple of Zion. In Zion, there will be a place called the New Jerusalem. That is a particular city in Zion where God will dwell in divinity. No one will see moon or sun in the city of God, for the glory of God will be the shining and lighting of the kingdom. Zion will be a much-arranged kingdom. There will be cities, which Jerusalem will be one of them. Verse 24 tells us that Zion will be arranged according to nations and those nations will be governed by kings. But those kings will be directly responsible to God.

They will all be subjected to the authority of the Father; all the nations of them that are saved shall walk in the light of it, and the kings of the earth do bring their glory and honor into it. Do not get it wrong: there will be demarcations as we have here on the face of the earth. We are not going to be in the same place. God is a god of order. Zion is surely going to be properly arranged and orderly governed by God. Verse 25 of the Revelation 21 tells that the gates of the cities of those nations will never be shut. "Its gates will never be shut by day, and there won't be any night." Thus, there will be no boundary barrier, of course; there will be no night in the kingdom. The glory and honor of the New Jerusalem will be in all the cities of the nations. The glory and honor of those cities of those nations will be brought to the New Jerusalem.

The Holy Ghost will be in the New Jerusalem. Revelation 22 describes the river of the water of life as clean as crystal, flowing from the throne of God and of the Lamb down to the middle of the great street of the city; there are names of streets in Zion. In Zion, there definitely is the ministry of the Holy Ghost. Zion will not be a boring place. It will be divinely glorified. The excess of living is the glorious life in the eternity.